HOLY COMMUNION AND WORSHIP OF THE EUCHARISTIC MYSTERY OUTSIDE MASS

THE ROMAN RITUAL

RENEWED BY DECREE OF
THE MOST HOLY SECOND ECUMENICAL COUNCIL OF THE VATICAN
AND PROMULGATED BY AUTHORITY OF POPE PAUL VI

HOLY COMMUNION AND WORSHIP OF THE EUCHARISTIC MYSTERY OUTSIDE MASS

ENGLISH TRANSLATION ACCORDING
TO THE TYPICAL EDITION

For Use in the Dioceses of the United States of America

Approved by the
United States Conference of Catholic Bishops
and Confirmed by the Apostolic See

CATHOLIC BOOK PUBLISHING CORP.
NEW JERSEY

Concordat cum originali:
✠ Steven J. Lopes
Chairman, USCCB Committee on Divine Worship
after review by Rev. Dustin P. Dought
Executive Director, USCCB Secretariat of Divine Worship

Imprimatur:
✠ Kevin J. Sweeney, D.D.
Bishop of Paterson

May 9, 2024

T-648

ISBN 978-1-958237-68-7

Printed in Korea 26 SW 3

catholicbookpublishing.com

CONTENTS

SACRED CONGREGATION FOR DIVINE WORSHIP

Prot. n. 900/73

DECREE

As spiritual nourishment for the faithful and as a pledge of eternal life, Christ entrusted the Sacrament of the Eucharist to the Church, his beloved bride, which she always receives with faith and love.

The celebration of the Eucharist in the Sacrifice of the Mass is truly the origin and purpose of the worship that is shown to the Eucharist outside Mass. The sacred species are reserved after Mass, particularly so that the faithful, especially the sick and the aged who are not able to be present at Mass, may be united with Christ and his Sacrifice that is offered in the Mass through sacramental Communion.

The reservation of the sacred species, which became customary in order to permit the reception of Communion, led to the custom of adoring this Sacrament and offering to it the worship that is due to God. This cult of adoration is based upon valid and solid principles. Moreover, some of its public and communal forms were instituted by the Church herself.

Therefore, with the revision of the Rite of the Mass and through the Instruction *Eucharisticum mysterium*, published on May 25, 1967, which laid down norms "on the practical arrangements for the worship due to this Sacrament even after Mass and its relationship to the proper ordering of the Sacrifice of the Mass in light of the instructions of the Second Vatican Council and of other documents of the Apostolic See on this matter,"[1] the Sacred Congregation for Divine Worship has revised the rites entitled, *De sacra communione et de cultu mysterii eucharistici extra Missam.*

These rites, approved by Pope Paul VI, are now published in this edition, which is declared to be the *editio typica*, to take the place of the rites that at present appear in the Roman Ritual. They may be used immediately in the Latin language and in the vernacular language, from the day which the Conferences of Bishops shall decree, after they have prepared a vernacular version and obtained the confirmation of the Apostolic See.

All things to the contrary notwithstanding.

From the offices of the Sacred Congregation for Divine Worship, June 21, 1973, on the Solemnity of the Most Holy Body and Blood of Christ.

Arturo Cardinal Tabera
Prefect

✠ A. Bugnini
Titular Archbishop of Diocletiana
Secretary

[1]Sacred Congregation of Rites, Instruction *Eucharisticum mysterium*, no. 3g: *Acta Apostolicæ Sedis* 59 (1967), p. 543.

DICASTERIUM DE CULTU DIVINO
ET DISCIPLINA SACRAMENTORUM

Prot. n. 99/22

CIVITATUM FŒDERATARUM AMERICÆ SEPTENTRIONALIS

Instante Excellentissimo Domino Iosepho Horatio Gomez, Archiepiscopo Angelorum in California, tunc Conferentiæ Episcoporum Civitatum Fœderatarum Americæ Septentrionalis Præside, litteris die 31 mensis ianuarii 2022 datis, vigore facultatum huic Dicasterio a Summo Pontifice FRANCISCO tributarum, textum translationis *anglicæ*, cum legitimis aptationibus recognitis, partis Ritualis Romani cui titulus est *De sacra communione et de cultu mysterii eucharistici extra Missam*, ab eadem Conferentia Episcoporum ad normam iuris die 17 mensis novembris anno 2021 approbatum, prout in adiecto exstat exemplari, perlibenter probamus et confirmamus.

In textu imprimendo inseratur ex integro hoc Decretum, quo ab Apostolica Sede petitæ confirmatio et recognitio conceduntur.

Eiusdem insuper textus impressi duo exemplaria ad hanc Dicasterium transmittantur.

Contrariis quibuslibet minime obstantibus.

Ex ædibus Dicasterii de Cultu Divino et Disciplina Sacramentorum, die 7 mensis martii 2023, in memoria Ss. Perpetuæ et Felicitatis, martyrum.

ARTURUS Card. ROCHE
Præfectus

✠ VICTORIUS FRANCISCUS VIOLA, O.F.M.
Archiepiscopus a Secretis

UNITED STATES CONFERENCE OF CATHOLIC BISHOPS

DECREE OF PROMULGATION

In accord with the norms established by the Holy See, this edition of *Holy Communion and Worship of the Eucharistic Mystery outside Mass* is declared to be the definitive approved English translation of *De sacra communione et de cultu mysterii eucharistici extra Missam, editio typica* (1973), and is hereby promulgated by authority of the United States Conference of Catholic Bishops.

Holy Communion and Worship of the Eucharistic Mystery outside Mass was canonically approved for use by the United States Conference of Catholic Bishops on November 17, 2021, and was subsequently confirmed by the Apostolic See by decree of the Dicastery for Divine Worship and the Discipline of the Sacraments on March 7, 2023 (Prot. n. 99/22).

This rite may be used in the Liturgy as of September 14, 2024, the Feast of the Exaltation of the Holy Cross, and its use is obligatory as of the First Sunday of Advent, December 1, 2024. From that date forward, no other English translation of the rite may be used in the dioceses of the United States of America.

Given at the General Secretariat of the United States Conference of Catholic Bishops, Washington, DC, on January 25, 2024, the Feast of the Conversion of Saint Paul the Apostle.

✠ Timothy P. Broglio
Archbishop for the Military Services, USA
President, United States Conference of Catholic Bishops

Rev. Michael J.K. Fuller
General Secretary

Α Ω

HOLY COMMUNION AND WORSHIP OF THE EUCHARISTIC MYSTERY OUTSIDE MASS

GENERAL INTRODUCTION

I. The Relationship between Eucharistic Worship outside Mass and the Eucharistic Celebration

1. The celebration of the Eucharist is the center of the whole Christian life, both for the universal Church and for local congregations of the same Church. For "the other Sacraments, as also all the ministries of the Church, and the works of the apostolate, are united with the Holy Eucharist and are directed toward it. For in the Most Holy Eucharist is contained all the spiritual wealth of the Church, that is, Christ himself, our Passover and living bread, through his flesh, made living and life-giving by the Holy Spirit, offering life to all, who are thus invited and led to offer themselves, their works, and all created things in union with him."[1]

2. Moreover, "the celebration of the Eucharist in the Sacrifice of the Mass is truly the origin and purpose of the worship that is shown to the Eucharist outside Mass."[2] For Christ the Lord "is offered in the Sacrifice of the Mass itself when he begins to be present sacramentally as spiritual food for the faithful under the species of bread and wine," and furthermore "after the Sacrifice has been offered, and when the Eucharist is reserved in churches or oratories, it is truly Emmanuel, that is, 'God with us.' For he is in our midst day and night and dwells in us, full of grace and truth."[3]

3. Let no one therefore doubt "that all the Christian faithful should show the worship and adoration that is truly due to God, in veneration of this Most Holy Sacrament, as has always been the custom in the Catholic Church. Nor should it be less adored, because it was instituted by Christ the Lord to be received as food."[4]

4. In order to direct and encourage devotion to the Most Holy Sacrament of the Eucharist correctly, the Eucharistic mystery must be considered in all its fullness, both in the celebration of the Mass and in the worship of the sacred species, which are reserved after Mass to extend the grace of the Sacrifice.[5]

---

[1] Second Vatican Council, Decree on the Ministry and Life of Priests, *Presbyterorum ordinis*, no. 5.

[2] Sacred Congregation of Rites, Instruction *Eucharisticum mysterium*, no. 3e: *Acta Apostolicæ Sedis* 59 (1967), p. 542.

[3] *Ibidem*, no. 3b: *loc. cit.*, p. 541; Paul VI, Encyclical Letter *Mysterium fidei*, near the end: *Acta Apostolicæ Sedis* 57 (1965), p. 771.

[4] Sacred Congregation of Rites, Instruction *Eucharisticum mysterium*, no. 3f: *Acta Apostolicæ Sedis* 59 (1967), p. 543.

[5] Cf. *ibidem*, no. 3g: *loc. cit.*, p. 543.

II. The Purpose of Reserving the Eucharist

5. The principal and original purpose of reserving the Eucharist outside Mass is the administration of Viaticum; the secondary purposes are the distribution of Communion and the adoration of our Lord Jesus Christ, present in the Sacrament. And indeed the reservation of the sacred species for the sick led to the praiseworthy custom of the adoration of this heavenly banquet which is kept in places of worship. And this cult of adoration is based on firm and solid reasoning, above all, because faith in the Real Presence of the Lord leads naturally to the external and public expression of that faith.[6]

6. In the celebration of the Mass, the principal ways in which Christ is present in the Church gradually become clear. First, he is present in the assembly of the faithful itself, gathered in his name; then in his word, when the Scriptures are read and expounded in church; also in the person of the minister; finally and above all, in the Eucharistic species. Indeed, in the Sacrament of the Eucharist, in an altogether unique way, the whole and entire Christ, God and man, is substantially and permanently present. This presence of Christ in the species "is called real, not by way of exclusion, as if other kinds of presence were not real, but because it is real *par excellence.*"[7]

Therefore, for the sake of the sign, it is more in keeping with the nature of the sacred celebration that, as far as possible, already from the beginning of the Mass, the sacred species should not be reserved in a tabernacle on the altar where the Mass is being celebrated, since the Eucharistic Presence of Christ is the fruit of the Consecration and should appear as such.[8]

7. The consecrated hosts, sufficient in number for the Communion of the sick and other faithful, should be frequently renewed and reserved in a pyx or other vessel.[9]

8. Pastors should see that, unless a grave reason stands in the way, churches where, in conformity with the law, the Most Holy Eucharist is reserved, are open every day for at least several hours at a convenient time, so that the faithful may easily pray in the presence of the Most Blessed Sacrament.[10]

---

[6] Cf. *ibidem*, no. 49: *loc. cit.*, pp. 566-567.

[7] Paul VI, Encyclical Letter *Mysterium fidei*: *Acta Apostolicæ Sedis* 57 (1965), p. 764; cf. Sacred Congregation of Rites, Instruction *Eucharisticum mysterium*, no. 9: *Acta Apostolicæ Sedis* 59 (1967), p. 547.

[8] Cf. Sacred Congregation of Rites, Instruction *Eucharisticum mysterium*, no. 55: *Acta Apostolicæ Sedis* 59 (1967), pp. 568-569.

[9] Cf. *Missale Romanum, editio typica tertia emendata* (2008), *Institutio generalis*, nos. 323 and 329.

[10] Cf. Sacred Congregation of Rites, Instruction *Eucharisticum mysterium*, no. 51: *Acta Apostolicæ Sedis* 59 (1967), p. 567; *Code of Canon Law*, can. 937.

III. The Place for the Reservation of the Eucharist

9. The Most Holy Eucharist should be reserved in a truly prominent place. It is strongly recommended that it also be suitable for private adoration and prayer, so that the faithful may never cease to honor the Lord present in the Sacrament, easily and fruitfully, in private worship.

This will be more easily achieved if the chapel is separate from the main body of the church, especially in those churches where weddings and funerals take place more frequently, and in those that are visited by many on account of pilgrimages or of artistic or historical treasures.

10. The Most Holy Eucharist should be reserved in a tabernacle that is irremovable, solid, not transparent, and locked in such a way that the danger of profanation is prevented to the greatest extent possible. Ordinarily there should be a single tabernacle in individual churches and oratories. The tabernacle is to be placed in a prominent and conspicuous part of the church that is worthily decorated and suitable for prayer.

The one in charge of the church or oratory should see to it that the key to the tabernacle where the Most Holy Eucharist is reserved is safeguarded most carefully.[11]

11. The presence of the Most Holy Eucharist in the tabernacle is indicated by a veil or in some other suitable way determined by the competent authority.

Near the tabernacle, in which the Most Holy Eucharist is reserved, a special lamp should shine continuously to indicate the presence of Christ and to honor it.

In accordance with traditional custom, the lamp should be fueled by oil or wax.[12]

IV. Those Things within the Competence of the Conferences of Bishops

12. It is within the competence of the Conferences of Bishops, in preparing particular Rituals in accordance with the *Constitution on the Sacred Liturgy* (no. 63b), to adapt this portion of the Roman Ritual to the needs of individual regions, so that, when their decisions have been accorded the *recognitio* of the Apostolic See, it may be used in the relevant regions.

In this matter it will be for the Conferences of Bishops:

[11] Cf. *ibidem*, nos. 52-53: *loc. cit.*, pp. 567-568; *Code of Canon Law*, can. 938.

[12] Cf. *ibidem*, no. 57: *loc. cit.*, p. 569; *Code of Canon Law*, can. 940.

a) to consider carefully and prudently which elements, if any, of popular traditions should be retained or admitted, provided that they can be reconciled with the spirit of the Sacred Liturgy; and then to propose to the Apostolic See the adaptations that they judge to be useful or necessary, and, after they have been accorded the *recognitio*, to introduce them.

b) to prepare translations of texts, so that they may be truly adapted to the character of the different languages and to the character of the cultures, and also to approve them, once their decisions have been accorded the *confirmatio* of the Apostolic See; to prepare and approve other texts according to the norm of law, especially for singing.

N.B. The liturgical texts which refer to males may be adapted to females, changing the gender, or to several people, changing the number.

CHAPTER I

HOLY COMMUNION OUTSIDE MASS

INTRODUCTION

I. The Relationships That Exist between Communion outside Mass and the Sacrifice

13. Sacramental Communion received within Mass is the more perfect participation in the Eucharistic Celebration. The Eucharistic sign is expressed more clearly, when the faithful receive the Body of the Lord after the Communion of the Priest, from the same Sacrifice.[1] Therefore recently made bread should be consecrated in every Eucharistic Celebration for the Communion of the faithful.

14. The faithful should be encouraged to receive Communion during the Eucharistic Celebration itself.

Priests, however, should not refuse to give Holy Communion to the faithful who for a just cause seek it, even outside Mass.[2]

In fact, it is fitting that those who are prevented from being present in the Eucharistic community should be diligently refreshed by the Eucharist, and in this way they may feel themselves united, not only with the Sacrifice of the Lord but also with the community itself, and supported by the love of their brothers and sisters.

Pastors of souls should take care that the sick and aged, even if not gravely sick or in imminent danger of death, should be given the opportunity to receive the Eucharist frequently, even, insofar as possible, daily, especially during Easter Time. Furthermore, it is permitted to administer the Eucharist under the species of wine alone, to those who are unable to receive under the species of bread.[3]

15. The faithful are to be carefully taught that, even when they receive Communion outside the celebration of Mass, they are intimately united with the Sacrifice which perpetuates the Sacrifice of the Cross, and they are participants in that sacred banquet in which, "by Communion in the Body and Blood of the Lord, the People of God participates in the blessings of the Paschal Sacrifice, renews the New Covenant made once by God with men in the Blood of Christ, and in faith and hope prefigures and anticipates the eschatological banquet in the Kingdom of the Father, proclaiming the Death of the Lord until he comes."[4]

---

[1] Cf. Second Vatican Council, Constitution on the Sacred Liturgy, *Sacrosanctum Concilium*, no. 55: *Acta Apostolicæ Sedis* 56 (1964), p. 115.

[2] Cf. Sacred Congregation of Rites, Instruction *Eucharisticum mysterium*, no. 33a: *Acta Apostolicæ Sedis* 59 (1967), pp. 559-560.

[3] Cf. *ibidem*, nos. 40-41: *loc. cit.*, pp. 562-563.

[4] *Ibidem*, no. 3a: *loc. cit.*, pp. 541-542.

II. The Time for Administering Holy Communion outside Mass

16. Holy Communion may be given outside Mass on any day and at any time of the day. It is proper, however, to determine times for the distribution of Holy Communion, bearing in mind the convenience of the faithful, so that the sacred celebration may be enacted in a fuller form, for the greater spiritual benefit of the faithful.

Nevertheless:

a) on Thursday of Holy Week, Holy Communion may be distributed only during Mass; it may, however, be brought to the sick at any time of the day;

b) on Good Friday of the Passion of the Lord, Holy Communion is distributed only during the celebration of the Passion of the Lord; but it may, however, be brought to the sick, who cannot take part in the celebration, at any time of the day;

c) on Holy Saturday, Holy Communion may be given only as Viaticum.[5]

III. The Minister of Holy Communion

17. It is first of all for the Priest or Deacon to administer Holy Communion to the faithful who ask for it.[6] It is in every way proper, therefore, that they should give part of their time to the performance of this ministry, according to the needs of the faithful.

Moreover, it is for a duly instituted acolyte, as an extraordinary minister, to give Holy Communion whenever there is no Priest or Deacon, either because of sickness, old age, or because they are prevented by pastoral duties or the number of faithful coming to the holy table is so great that the celebration of the Mass or other sacred celebration may be greatly prolonged.[7]

The local Ordinary may give the faculty of distributing Holy Communion to other extraordinary ministers, whenever it may seem necessary for the pastoral benefit of the faithful, and a Priest or Deacon or acolyte is not available.[8]

[5] Cf. *Missale Romanum, editio typica tertia emendata* (2008), *Ad Missam vespertinam*, no. 4; *Celebratio Passionis Domini*, no. 2; *Sabbato sancto*, no. 3.

[6] Cf. Sacred Congregation of Rites, Instruction *Eucharisticum mysterium*, no. 31: *Acta Apostolicæ Sedis* 59 (1967), pp. 557-558.

[7] Cf. Paul VI, Apostolic Letter *Ministeria quædam*, August 15, 1972, no. VI: *Acta Apostolicæ Sedis* 64 (1972), p. 532.

[8] Cf. Sacred Congregation for the Discipline of the Sacraments, Instruction *Immensæ caritatis*, January 29, 1973, 1, I and II: *Acta Apostolicæ Sedis* 65 (1973), pp. 265-266.

IV. The Place for Distributing Communion outside Mass

18. The place in which Holy Communion is normally given outside Mass is a church or oratory in which the Eucharist is regularly celebrated or reserved, or a church or oratory or other place in which the local community habitually comes together for the liturgical assembly on Sundays or other days. However, Holy Communion may be given in other places, not excluding private houses, when the sick, prisoners, or others involved cannot leave the place without danger or grave difficulty.

V. Norms Governing the Distribution of Holy Communion

19. When Holy Communion is administered in a church or oratory, a corporal should be placed on the altar, which is already covered with a cloth; two candles should be lit, as a sign of veneration and of the festive banquet.[9] A paten should be used.

But when Holy Communion is administered in other places, a suitable table is prepared, covered with a cloth; candles should also be provided.

20. The minister of Holy Communion, if he is a Priest or Deacon, should be vested in an alb, or a surplice over a cassock, and should wear a stole.

Other ministers should wear either the liturgical vesture traditional in their region or vesture which is not unsuitable for this ministry and is approved by the Ordinary.

The Eucharist for administering Communion outside the church should be carried in a pyx or other closed vessel, with such coverings and in such a manner as is appropriate to the place.

21. In distributing Holy Communion the custom of placing a particle of consecrated bread on the tongue of the communicant is to be observed, because it is based on a tradition of several centuries.

However, the Conferences of Bishops may determine, when their decisions have been confirmed by the Apostolic See, that in their jurisdiction, Holy Communion may be distributed by placing the consecrated bread in the hands of the faithful, provided that due care is taken that no lack of reverence or false opinions about the Most Holy Eucharist should insinuate themselves into the minds of the faithful.[10]

---

[9] Cf. *Missale Romanum, editio typica tertia emendata* (2008), *Institutio generalis*, no. 307.

[10] Cf. Sacred Congregation for Divine Worship, Instruction *Memoriale Domini*, May 29, 1969: *Acta Apostolicæ Sedis* 61 (1969), pp. 541-555.

Moreover, the faithful should be taught that Jesus Christ is Lord and Savior and that, present in the sacramental species, he should be given the same worship or adoration that is due to God.[11]

In either case, Communion should be given by the competent minister, who shows the particle of consecrated bread to the communicant and gives it to him (her), saying the words, The Body of Christ, to which the communicant replies, Amen.

With regard to what pertains to the distribution of Holy Communion under the species of wine, the liturgical norms should be observed exactly.[12]

22. Fragments that may remain after Communion should be reverently collected and placed in a pyx or put into a vessel with water.

Similarly, if Communion is administered under the species of wine, the chalice or other vessel used for this purpose should be washed with water.

The water used for the ablutions may be either drunk or poured out in an appropriate place.

VI. Dispositions for Receiving Holy Communion

23. The Eucharist, which continuously represents the Paschal Mystery of Christ in the midst of humanity, is the fount of all grace and of the remission of sins. Nevertheless, those who intend to receive the Body of the Lord, should come to it with clean consciences and properly disposed souls, so that they may harvest the fruits of the paschal Sacrament.

The Church therefore teaches "that no one conscious of mortal sin in themselves, however contrite they feel themselves to be, should receive the Holy Eucharist without previous sacramental confession."[13] If there is a serious reason and no opportunity for confession, they should make an act of perfect contrition with the intention of confessing individually, as soon as possible, the mortal sins that they cannot confess at present.

---

[11] Cf. Sacred Congregation for the Discipline of the Sacraments, Instruction *Immensæ caritatis*, January 29, 1973, no. 4: *Acta Apostolicæ Sedis* 65 (1973), p. 270.

[12] Cf. *Missale Romanum, editio typica tertia emendata* (2008), *Institutio generalis*, no. 283; cf. Sacred Congregation for Divine Worship, Instruction *Sacramentali Communione*, June 29, 1970, no. 6: *Acta Apostolicæ Sedis* 62 (1970), pp. 665-666.

[13] Cf. Council of Trent, Session XIII, *Decretum de ss. Eucharistiæ sacramento*, cap. 7: Denzinger-Schönmetzer 1646-1647; *ibidem*, Session XIV, *Canones de sacramento Pœnitentiæ*, can. 9: Denzinger-Schönmetzer 1709; Sacred Congregation for the Doctrine of the Faith, *Pastoral Norms for the Administration of General Sacramental Absolution*, June 16, 1972, Introduction and no. VI: *Acta Apostolicæ Sedis* 64 (1972), pp. 510 and 512.

It is desirable that those who are accustomed to communicate daily or quite often go to the Sacrament of Penance at regular intervals, depending on their circumstances.

Moreover, the faithful should look on the Eucharist as an antidote that frees them from daily faults and preserves them from mortal sins; in addition, they should understand the right way to use the penitential parts of the liturgy, especially of the Mass.[14]

24. Communicants should not receive the Sacrament unless they have fasted for at least one hour from food and drink, with the sole exceptions of water and medicine.

The elderly and those suffering from any kind of infirmity, as well as those who take care of such persons, may receive the Most Holy Eucharist even if they have consumed something within the hour before.[15]

25. Union with Christ, to which the Sacrament itself is directed, should be extended to the whole Christian life, so that the Christian faithful, continually contemplating the gift they have received, live their daily lives under the guidance of the Holy Spirit, as an act of thanksgiving, and bring forth more abundantly the fruits of charity.

In order that they may more easily continue the act of thanksgiving which is offered to God in a splendid way in the Mass, it is recommended that all who have been refreshed in Holy Communion should continue in prayer for a certain period of time.[16]

[14]Cf. Sacred Congregation of Rites, Instruction *Eucharisticum mysterium*, no. 35: *Acta Apostolicæ Sedis* 59 (1967), p. 561.

[15]Cf. *Code of Canon Law*, can. 919 §§ 1 and 3.

[16]Cf. Sacred Congregation of Rites, Instruction *Eucharisticum mysterium*, no. 38: *Acta Apostolicæ Sedis* 59 (1967), p. 562.

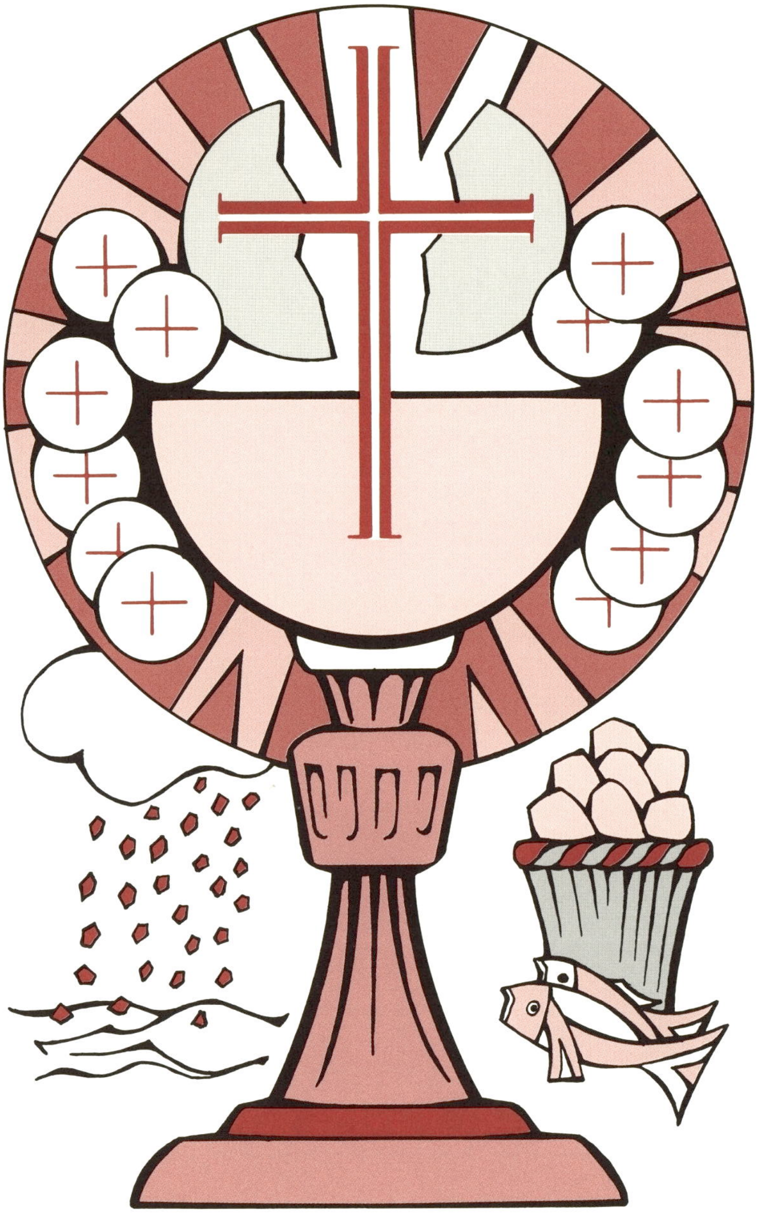

THE ORDER OF DISTRIBUTING HOLY COMMUNION OUTSIDE MASS

I. The Rite with a Fuller Celebration of the Word of God

26. This form is to be used especially when the celebration of Mass has not taken place or when Holy Communion is distributed at scheduled times, so that the faithful may also be nourished from the table of the word of God. For by hearing the word of God, the faithful themselves understand that God's wonders, which are being proclaimed, reach their preeminence in the Paschal Mystery, the memorial of which is celebrated sacramentally in the Mass, and in which they participate by Communion. Moreover, receiving the word of the Lord and being nourished by it, they are led on, in thanksgiving, to fruitful participation in the mysteries of salvation.

The Introductory Rites

27. When the faithful are gathered and everything has been arranged as noted above (nos. 19-20), the minister begins with the Sign of the Cross, then greets those present.

If he is a Priest or Deacon, he says:

The grace of our Lord Jesus Christ,
and the love of God,
and the communion of the Holy Spirit
be with you all.

All reply:

And with your spirit.

Or:

The Lord be with you.

All reply:

And with your spirit.

If, however, the minister is not a Priest or Deacon, he (she) greets those present with these or similar words:

Bless the Lord, brothers and sisters,
who in his goodness invites us (you)
to the table of the Body of Christ.

All reply:

Blessed be God for ever.

Another optional formula of greeting, no. 189.

Other words from Sacred Scripture, with which the faithful are customarily greeted, may also be used.

28. The Penitential Act then occurs. The minister invites the communicants to repentance, saying:

Brethren (Brothers and sisters), let us acknowledge our sins, and so prepare ourselves to participate in this sacred celebration.

A brief pause for silence follows. Then all recite together the I confess:

I confess to almighty God
and to you, my brothers and sisters,
that I have greatly sinned,
in my thoughts and in my words,
in what I have done and in what I have failed to do,

And, striking their breast, they say:

through my fault, through my fault,
through my most grievous fault;

Then they continue:

therefore I ask blessed Mary ever-Virgin,
all the Angels and Saints,
and you, my brothers and sisters,
to pray for me to the Lord our God.

The minister concludes:

**May almighty God have mercy on us,
forgive us our sins,
and bring us to everlasting life.**

All reply:

Amen.

Other optional formulas of the Penitential Act, nos. 190-191.

The Celebration of the Word of God

29. Then the celebration of the word occurs, which takes place in the same manner as at Mass. Texts are chosen, as appropriate, either from the liturgy of the day or from the readings proposed for the Votive Masses of the Most Holy Eucharist (*Lectionary for Mass*, nos. 976-981) or of the Most Precious Blood of our Lord Jesus Christ (*Lectionary for Mass*, nos. 989-994), and which are indicated at nos. 113-153 of this Ritual. Other texts for special circumstances may also be chosen, as appropriate, from the *Lectionary*, especially readings from the Votive Mass of the Most Sacred Heart of Jesus (nos. 995-1000), as indicated at nos. 154-188 below.

One or more readings, however, may be used according to what may seem appropriate. After the First Reading, a psalm or some other chant may occur or, in its place, a period of sacred silence may even be observed.

The celebration of the word is concluded with the Universal Prayer (Prayer of the Faithful).

Holy Communion

30. When the Universal Prayer (Prayer of the Faithful) is concluded, the minister approaches the place where the Eucharist is reserved, takes the vessel or ciborium containing the Body of the Lord, places it on the altar, and genuflects. The minister then introduces the Lord's Prayer in these or similar words:

**At the Savior's command
and formed by divine teaching,
we dare to say:**

And all together continue:

**Our Father, who art in heaven,
hallowed be thy name;
thy kingdom come,
thy will be done
on earth as it is in heaven.
Give us this day our daily bread,
and forgive us our trespasses,
as we forgive those who trespass against us;
and lead us not into temptation,
but deliver us from evil.**

31. After this, the minister, if appropriate, invites the faithful in these or similar words:

Let us offer each other the sign of peace.

And all offer one another a sign, in keeping with local customs, that expresses peace and charity.

32. After this, the minister genuflects, takes the host and, holding it slightly raised above the vessel or ciborium, while facing the communicants, says:

**Behold the Lamb of God,
behold him who takes away the sins of the world.
Blessed are those called to the supper of the Lamb.**

And the communicants add once:

Lord, I am not worthy
that you should enter under my roof,
but only say the word
and my soul shall be healed.

33. If the minister receives Communion, he (she) says quietly:

May the Body of Christ
keep me safe for eternal life.

And he (she) reverently consumes the Body of Christ.

34. After this, the minister takes the vessel or ciborium and approaches the communicants. The minister raises a host slightly and shows it to each of the communicants, saying:

The Body of Christ.

The communicant replies:

Amen.

And receives Holy Communion.

35. While the distribution of Communion takes place, an appropriate liturgical song may be sung.

36. When the distribution of Communion is complete, the minister puts any fragments which may perhaps be found on the paten into the ciborium, and if appropriate may wash his (her) hands. If there are a number of hosts, however, the minister returns the Sacrament to the tabernacle and genuflects.

37. Then, if appropriate, a sacred silence may be observed for a while, or a psalm or canticle of praise may be sung.

38. The minister then says the concluding prayer:

Let us pray.

O God, who in this wonderful Sacrament
have left us a memorial of your Passion,
grant us, we pray,
so to revere the sacred mysteries of your Body and Blood
that we may always experience in ourselves
the fruits of your redemption.
Who live and reign for ever and ever.

All reply:

Amen.

Other optional prayers, nos. 210-219.

During Easter Time, however, the prayers indicated in nos. 220-222 are to be said.

The Concluding Rites

39. Then the minister, if he is a Priest or Deacon, facing the people and extending his hands, says:

The Lord be with you.

All

And with your spirit.

And he blesses the people, saying:

May almighty God bless you,
the Father, and the Son, ✠ and the Holy Spirit.

All reply:

Amen.

In place of this formula, a Solemn Blessing or Prayer over the People may also be used, as occurs at the end of Mass in the *Roman Missal*.

---

40. If, however, the minister is neither a Priest nor a Deacon, while invoking God's blessing and signing himself (herself), he (she) says:

May the Lord bless us,
protect us from all evil
and lead us to everlasting life.

Or:

May the almighty and merciful Lord bless us and keep us,
the Father, and the Son, and the Holy Spirit.

All reply:

Amen.

---

41. Finally, the minister says:

Go in peace.

All reply:

Thanks be to God.

Then, after making an appropriate sign of reverence, the minister leaves.

II. The Rite with a Brief Celebration of the Word of God

42. This form is used when circumstances suggest that the form combined with a fuller celebration of the word of God is not appropriate, especially when there are only one or two communicants and, therefore, a celebration of the community cannot be arranged.

The Introductory Rites

43. When everything has been arranged as above (nos. 19-20), the minister greets the communicants (nos. 27, 189) and invites them to take part in the Penitential Act (nos. 28, 190-191).

The Shorter Reading of the Word of God

44. Then, omitting the celebration of the word of God, a short text of Sacred Scripture, in which there should be a mention of the Bread of Life, may be read as appropriate by one of those present or by the minister.

John 6:54-55

Whoever eats my Flesh and drinks my Blood
has eternal life,
and I will raise him on the last day.
For my Flesh is true food,
and my Blood is true drink.

John 6:54-58

Whoever eats my Flesh and drinks my Blood
has eternal life,
and I will raise him on the last day.
For my Flesh is true food,
and my Blood is true drink.
Whoever eats my Flesh and drinks my Blood
remains in me and I in him.
Just as the living Father sent me
and I have life because of the Father,

so also the one who feeds on me
will have life because of me.
This is the bread that came down from heaven.
Unlike your ancestors who ate and still died,
whoever eats this bread will live forever.

John 14:6

I am the way and the truth and the life.
No one comes to the Father except through me.

John 14:23

Whoever loves me will keep my word,
and my Father will love him,
and we will come to him and make our dwelling with him.

John 15:4

Remain in me, as I remain in you.
Just as a branch cannot bear fruit on its own
unless it remains on the vine,
so neither can you unless you remain in me.

1 Corinthians 11:26

As often as you eat this bread and drink the cup,
you proclaim the death of the Lord until he comes.

Other appropriate texts may also be chosen from those noted below, nos. 113 ff.

Holy Communion

45. The minister takes the vessel or ciborium containing the Body of the Lord, places it on the altar, and genuflects. The minister then introduces the Lord's Prayer in these or similar words:

At the Savior's command
and formed by divine teaching,
we dare to say:

And all together continue:

Our Father, who art in heaven,
hallowed be thy name;
thy kingdom come,
thy will be done
on earth as it is in heaven.
Give us this day our daily bread,
and forgive us our trespasses,
as we forgive those who trespass against us;
and lead us not into temptation,
but deliver us from evil.

46. After this, the minister genuflects, takes the host and, holding it slightly raised above the vessel or ciborium, while facing the communicants, says:

Behold the Lamb of God,
behold him who takes away the sins of the world.
Blessed are those called to the supper of the Lamb.

And the communicants add once:

Lord, I am not worthy
that you should enter under my roof,
but only say the word
and my soul shall be healed.

47. If the minister receives Communion, he (she) says quietly:

May the Body of Christ
keep me safe for eternal life.

And he (she) reverently consumes the Body of Christ.

48. After this, the minister takes the vessel or ciborium and approaches the communicants. The minister raises a host slightly and shows it to each of the communicants, saying:

The Body of Christ.

The communicant replies:

Amen.

And receives Holy Communion.

49. When the distribution of Communion is complete, the minister puts any fragments which may perhaps be found on the paten into the ciborium, and if appropriate may wash his (her) hands. If there are a number of hosts, however, the minister returns the Sacrament to the tabernacle and genuflects.

Then, if appropriate, a sacred silence may be observed for a while, or a psalm or canticle of praise may be sung.

50. The minister then says the concluding prayer:

Let us pray.

O God, who in this wonderful Sacrament
have left us a memorial of your Passion,
grant us, we pray,
so to revere the sacred mysteries of your Body and Blood
that we may always experience in ourselves
the fruits of your redemption.
Who live and reign for ever and ever.

All reply:

Amen.

Other optional prayers, nos. 210-219.

During Easter Time, however, the prayers indicated in nos. 220-222 are to be said.

The Concluding Rites

51. Then the minister, if he is a Priest or Deacon, facing the people and extending his hands, says:

The Lord be with you.

All

And with your spirit.

And he blesses the people, saying:

May almighty God bless you,
the Father, and the Son, ✠ and the Holy Spirit.

All reply:

Amen.

52. If, however, the minister is neither a Priest nor a Deacon, while invoking God's blessing and signing himself (herself), he (she) says:

May the Lord bless us,
protect us from all evil
and lead us to everlasting life.

Or:

May the almighty and merciful Lord bless us and keep us,
the Father, and the Son, and the Holy Spirit.

All reply:

Amen.

53. Finally, the minister says:

Go in peace.

All reply:

Thanks be to God.

Then, after making an appropriate sign of reverence, the minister leaves.

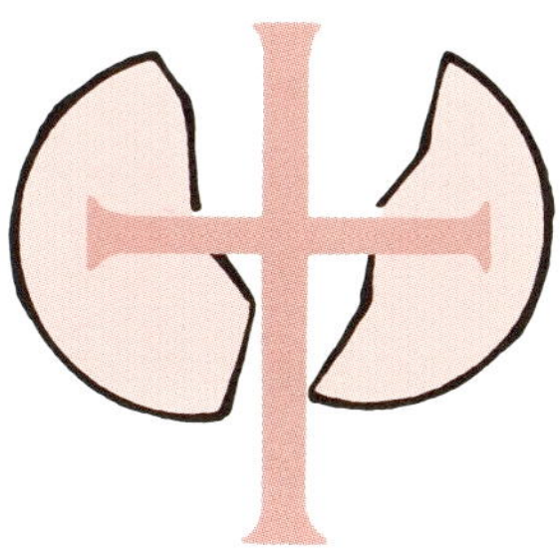

CHAPTER II

ADMINISTRATION OF COMMUNION AND VIATICUM TO THE SICK BY AN EXTRAORDINARY MINISTER

54. A Priest or Deacon administers Holy Communion and Viaticum to the sick according to the rites in *The Order of the Anointing of the Sick and of their Pastoral Care*. When, however, the Most Holy Eucharist is brought to the sick by an acolyte or an extraordinary minister of Holy Communion deputed in accordance with the norm of law, the rites that follow are to be observed.

55. It is permitted to administer the Eucharist under the species of wine alone to those who are unable to receive it under the species of bread.

The Blood of the Lord must be carried to the sick person in a vessel so closed as to avoid completely any danger of spillage. In administering the Sacrament, however, the more appropriate manner should be chosen, in each case, from those proposed for distributing Communion under both kinds. When Communion is completed, if any of the Most Precious Blood remains, it should be consumed by the minister, who should also take care of the necessary purifications.

I. The Ordinary Rite of Communion of the Sick

The Introductory Rites

56. Wearing vestments appropriate for this ministry (cf. no. 20), after approaching the sick person, the minister warmly greets them and the others present, using, if appropriate, the greeting:

Peace to this house and all here.

Other words from Sacred Scripture, with which the faithful are customarily greeted, may also be used.

Then, after placing the Sacrament on a table, the minister and all present adore it.

57. The minister invites the sick person and others present to take part in the Penitential Act:

Brethren (Brothers and sisters), let us acknowledge our sins, and so prepare ourselves to participate in this sacred celebration.

A brief pause for silence follows. Then all recite together the I confess:

I confess to almighty God
and to you, my brothers and sisters,
that I have greatly sinned,
in my thoughts and in my words,
in what I have done and in what I have failed to do,

And, striking their breast, they say:

through my fault, through my fault,
through my most grievous fault;

Then they continue:

therefore I ask blessed Mary ever-Virgin,
all the Angels and Saints,
and you, my brothers and sisters,
to pray for me to the Lord our God.

The minister concludes:

May almighty God have mercy on us,
forgive us our sins,
and bring us to everlasting life.

All reply:

Amen.

Other optional formulas of the Penitential Act, nos. 190-191.

The Shorter Reading of the Word of God

58. Then, a short text of Sacred Scripture, for example from those indicated below in no. 71, may be read as appropriate by one of those present or by the minister.

Holy Communion

59. Then the minister introduces the Lord's Prayer in these or similar words:

**Now let us together call upon God,
as our Lord Jesus Christ taught us to pray:**

And all together continue:

**Our Father, who art in heaven,
hallowed be thy name;
thy kingdom come,
thy will be done
on earth as it is in heaven.
Give us this day our daily bread,
and forgive us our trespasses,
as we forgive those who trespass against us;
and lead us not into temptation,
but deliver us from evil.**

60. Then the minister shows the Most Blessed Sacrament, saying:

**Behold the Lamb of God,
behold him who takes away the sins of the world.
Blessed are those called to the supper of the Lamb.**

The sick person and any others who will receive Communion say once:

Lord, I am not worthy
that you should enter under my roof,
but only say the word
and my soul shall be healed.

61. The minister approaches the sick person, and showing them the Sacrament, says:

The Body of Christ (or: **The Blood of Christ**).

The sick person replies:

Amen.

And receives Holy Communion.

Those present who wish to receive Communion receive the Sacrament in the usual way.

62. When the distribution of Communion is complete, the minister carries out the purification as usual. Then, if appropriate, a sacred silence may be observed for a while.

Then the minister says the concluding prayer:

Let us pray.

O Lord, holy Father, almighty and eternal God,
with faith we entreat you
that the most holy Body (most holy Blood)
of our Lord Jesus Christ your Son
may benefit our brother (sister) who receives it
as an everlasting remedy
for both body and soul.
Through Christ our Lord.

All reply:

Amen.

Other optional prayers, nos. 210-222.

The Concluding Rites

63. Then the minister, while invoking God's blessing and signing himself (herself), says:

May the Lord bless us,
protect us from all evil
and lead us to everlasting life.

Or:

May the almighty and merciful Lord bless us and keep us,
the Father, and the Son, and the Holy Spirit.

All reply:

Amen.

II. A Shorter Rite of Communion of the Sick

64. This shorter rite is used when Holy Communion is to be given to a number of the sick in different rooms of the same building, for example, to those staying in the same hospital. As the case requires, some elements taken from the ordinary rite may be added (nos. 56-63).

65. The rite may begin either in the church or chapel or in the first room, while the minister says this antiphon:

O sacred banquet, in which Christ is received:
the memory of his Passion is renewed,
the mind is filled with grace,
and a pledge of future glory is given to us.

Other optional antiphons, nos. 201-203.

66. Then the minister, accompanied by a person carrying a candle if appropriate, approaches the sick persons and says once to all the sick who are present in the same room or to each of the communicants individually:

Behold the Lamb of God,
behold him who takes away the sins of the world.
Blessed are those called to the supper of the Lamb.

And the communicants add once:

Lord, I am not worthy
that you should enter under my roof,
but only say the word
and my soul shall be healed.

And they receive Communion in the usual way.

67. The rite is concluded with a prayer (cf. no. 62) which may be said either in a church or a chapel or in the last room.

III. Viaticum

The Introductory Rites

68. Wearing vestments appropriate for this ministry (cf. no. 20), after approaching the sick person, the minister warmly greets them and the others present, using, if appropriate, the greeting:

Peace to this house and all here.

Other words from Sacred Scripture, with which the faithful are customarily greeted, may also be used.

Then, after placing the Sacrament on a table, the minister and all present adore it.

69. Afterwards, the minister addresses those present with the following introduction, or another one more suited to the sick person's conditions:

Dear brothers and sisters,
before he passed from this world to the Father,
the Lord Jesus Christ left us the Sacrament of his Body and Blood,
so that at the hour of our passing from this life to him,
we may be strengthened by the Viaticum of his Body and Blood
and be fortified with the pledge of resurrection.
United with our brother (sister) in charity,
let us pray for him (her).

And all pray in silence for a while.

70. The minister invites the sick person and others present to take part in the Penitential Act:

Brethren (Brothers and sisters), let us acknowledge our sins,
and so prepare ourselves to participate in this sacred celebration.

A brief pause for silence follows. Then all recite together the **I confess**:

I confess to almighty God
and to you, my brothers and sisters,
that I have greatly sinned,
in my thoughts and in my words,
in what I have done and in what I have failed to do,

And, striking their breast, they say:

through my fault, through my fault,
through my most grievous fault;

Then they continue:

therefore I ask blessed Mary ever-Virgin,
all the Angels and Saints,
and you, my brothers and sisters,
to pray for me to the Lord our God.

The minister concludes:

May almighty God have mercy on us,
forgive us our sins,
and bring us to everlasting life.

All reply:

Amen.

Other optional formulas of the Penitential Act, nos. **190-191**.

The Shorter Reading of the Word of God

71. It is very appropriate that one of those present or the minister read a brief text of Sacred Scripture, for example:

John 6:54-55

Whoever eats my Flesh and drinks my Blood
has eternal life,
and I will raise him on the last day.
For my Flesh is true food,
and my Blood is true drink.

John 6:54-58

Whoever eats my Flesh and drinks my Blood
has eternal life,
and I will raise him on the last day.
For my Flesh is true food,
and my Blood is true drink.
Whoever eats my Flesh and drinks my Blood
remains in me and I in him.
Just as the living Father sent me
and I have life because of the Father,
so also the one who feeds on me
will have life because of me.
This is the bread that came down from heaven.
Unlike your ancestors who ate and still died,
whoever eats this bread will live forever.

John 14:6

I am the way and the truth and the life.
No one comes to the Father except through me.

John 14:23

Whoever loves me will keep my word,
and my Father will love him,
and we will come to him and make our dwelling with him.

John 14:27

Peace I leave with you; my peace I give to you.
Not as the world gives do I give it to you.
Do not let your hearts be troubled or afraid.

John 15:4

Remain in me, as I remain in you.
Just as a branch cannot bear fruit on its own
unless it remains on the vine,
so neither can you unless you remain in me.

John 15:5

**I am the vine, you are the branches.
Whoever remains in me and I in him will bear much fruit,
because without me you can do nothing.**

1 Corinthians 11:26

**As often as you eat this bread and drink the cup,
you proclaim the death of the Lord until he comes.**

1 John 4:16

**We have come to know and to believe in the love God has for us.
God is love, and whoever remains in love
remains in God and God in him.**

Another appropriate text may also be chosen from those found in *The Order of the Anointing of the Sick and of their Pastoral Care* (nos. 247 ff. or 153 ff.).

The Profession of Baptismal Faith

72. It is desirable that the sick person, before receiving Viaticum, renew his (her) profession of baptismal faith. Then, the minister having offered a brief introduction with appropriate words, asks him (her):

**Do you believe in God,
the Father almighty,
Creator of heaven and earth?**

℟. I do.

Minister:

**Do you believe in Jesus Christ, his only Son, our Lord,
who was born of the Virgin Mary,
suffered death and was buried,
rose again from the dead
and is seated at the right hand of the Father?**

℟. I do.

Minister:

Do you believe in the Holy Spirit,
the holy catholic Church,
the communion of saints,
the forgiveness of sins,
the resurrection of the body,
and life everlasting?

℟. I do.

Prayer for the Sick Person

73. Then, if the condition of the sick person permits, a brief prayer takes place in these or similar words, with the sick person, insofar as possible, and those present responding:

Dear brothers and sisters,
with one heart let us invoke the Lord Jesus Christ:

—To you, O Lord, who loved us to the end
and handed yourself over to death in order to give us life,
we pray for our brother (sister).

℟. Hear us, O Lord.

—To you, O Lord, who said:
Whoever eats my Flesh and drinks my Blood has eternal life,
we pray for our brother (sister).

℟. Hear us, O Lord.

—To you, O Lord, who invite us to that banquet
where there will be no more pain or grief,
neither sadness, nor separation,
we pray for our brother (sister).

℟. Hear us, O Lord.

Viaticum

74. Then the minister introduces the Lord's Prayer in these or similar words:

Now let us together call upon God,
as our Lord Jesus Christ taught us to pray:

And all together continue:

Our Father, who art in heaven,
hallowed be thy name;
thy kingdom come,
thy will be done
on earth as it is in heaven.
Give us this day our daily bread,
and forgive us our trespasses,
as we forgive those who trespass against us;
and lead us not into temptation,
but deliver us from evil.

75. Then the minister shows the Most Blessed Sacrament, saying:

Behold the Lamb of God,
behold him who takes away the sins of the world.
Blessed are those called to the supper of the Lamb.

The sick person, if possible, and any others who will receive Communion say once:

Lord, I am not worthy
that you should enter under my roof,
but only say the word
and my soul shall be healed.

76. The minister approaches the sick person, and showing them the Sacrament, says:

The Body of Christ (or: **The Blood of Christ**).

The sick person replies:

Amen.

And immediately, or after giving Communion, the minister adds:

May he protect you and lead you to eternal life.

The sick person replies:

Amen.

Those present who wish to receive Communion receive the Sacrament in the usual way.

77. When the distribution of Communion is complete, the minister carries out the purification as usual. Then, if appropriate, a sacred silence may be observed for a while.

The Concluding Rites

78. Then the minister says the concluding prayer:

Let us pray.

O God, whose Son is for us the way, the truth and the life,
look lovingly upon your servant N.
and grant that, trusting in your promises
and strengthened by the Body and Blood of your Son,
he (she) may journey in peace to your Kingdom.
Through Christ our Lord.

All reply:

Amen.

Another optional prayer, no. 223.

Then the minister says:

May the Lord be with you always,
may he strengthen you by his power
and keep you in peace.

Then both the minister and those present may offer a Sign of Peace to the sick person.

CHAPTER III

VARIOUS FORMS OF WORSHIP OF THE MOST HOLY EUCHARIST

79. Since the Eucharistic Sacrifice is the source and summit of the whole Christian life, devotion, both private and public, to the Most Holy Eucharist, even outside Mass, is strongly recommended, according to the norms established by lawful authority.

When arranging pious and holy exercises of this kind, account should be taken of the liturgical seasons, so that these exercises are in harmony with the Sacred Liturgy from which, in a sense, they derive, and may lead the people back to it.[1]

80. When the faithful worship Christ present in the Sacrament, they should remember that this presence derives from the Sacrifice and tends toward sacramental and spiritual communion.

Therefore, the piety that moves the faithful to apply themselves to adore the Holy Eucharist attracts them to participate deeply in the Paschal Mystery and to respond with grateful hearts to the gift of him, who by his humanity continually pours his divine life into the members of his Body. Living with Christ the Lord, they enjoy an intimate familiarity with him and, in his presence, pour out their hearts for themselves and for all their loved ones, and pray for the peace and salvation of the world. Offering their whole lives with Christ to the Father in the Holy Spirit, they draw from this wonderful exchange an increase of faith and hope and love. In this way, therefore, they nourish the right dispositions, by which they are able to celebrate the memorial of the Lord with devotion and to receive frequently that Bread given to us by the Father.

The faithful should therefore strive to worship Christ the Lord in the Sacrament, according to the circumstances of their own life. Pastors, moreover, should lead them in this by their example and encourage them by their words.[2]

---

[1]Cf. Sacred Congregation of Rites, Instruction *Eucharisticum mysterium*, no. 58: *Acta Apostolicæ Sedis* 59 (1967), p. 569.

[2]Cf. *ibidem*, no. 50: *loc. cit.*, p. 567.

81. They should remember above all that in prayer of this sort before Christ the Lord, present in the Sacrament, they extend that union with him, which they have reached in Communion, and renew that covenant, which urges them to maintain in their morals and their life what they have received in the celebration of the Eucharist in faith and Sacrament. They should strive, therefore, to lead their whole life gladly in the strength of the heavenly food, as they participate in the Death and Resurrection of the Lord. Everyone, therefore, should be careful to perform good works and to please God, so as to imbue the world with the Christian spirit and to become a witness to Christ in the midst of human affairs.[3]

I. Exposition of the Most Holy Eucharist

INTRODUCTION

I. The Relationship That Exists between Exposition and the Mass

82. Exposition of the Most Holy Eucharist, whether in a ciborium or in a monstrance, encourages the acknowledgement of Christ's wonderful presence in it and invites us to a union of heart with him that reaches its summit in sacramental Communion. Therefore, it fosters very well the worship in spirit and in truth that is due to him.

Care should be taken that, in exposition of this kind, worship of the Most Blessed Sacrament should shed light on the relationship that it has with the Mass. In preparing exposition, everything should be carefully avoided which might in any way obscure the desire of Christ, who especially instituted the Most Holy Eucharist, that he might be close to us as food, medicine, and comfort.[4]

83. During exposition of the Most Blessed Sacrament, the celebration of Mass is prohibited in the same part of the church or oratory.

For, besides the reasons given in no. 6, the celebration of the Eucharistic Mystery includes in a more perfect way the interior communion to which exposition aims to lead the faithful.

If the exposition of the Most Blessed Sacrament is extended for one or more days subsequently, it is to be interrupted during the celebration of Mass, unless perhaps the Mass is celebrated in a chapel separate from the place of exposition and at least some of the faithful remain in adoration.[5]

[3]Cf. *ibidem*, no. 13: *loc. cit.*, p. 549.

[4]Cf. *ibidem*, no. 60: *loc. cit.*, p. 570.

[5]Cf. *ibidem*, no. 61: *loc. cit.*, pp. 570-571.

II. Points to Be Observed in Arranging Exposition

84. A single genuflection is made in the presence of the Most Blessed Sacrament, whether reserved in the tabernacle or exposed for public exposition.

85. When exposition of the Most Blessed Sacrament is conducted with a monstrance, four or six candles are lit, as at Mass, and incense is used. In exposition with a ciborium, at least two candles are lit; incense may be used.

Extended Exposition

86. In churches and oratories where the Eucharist is reserved, it is recommended that solemn exposition of the Most Blessed Sacrament for an extended period of time should take place once a year, even if not strictly continuously, so that the local community may meditate on and adore this mystery more profoundly.

This sort of exposition, however, may take place only if a suitable number of the faithful is expected to be present.[6]

87. For some serious and general need, the local Ordinary may order supplication, extended for a longer time, to be made before the Most Blessed Sacrament, in those churches where the faithful more frequently assemble.[7]

88. When, for want of ample numbers of worshipers, uninterrupted exposition is not possible, the Most Blessed Sacrament may be placed back in the tabernacle, at times scheduled and announced beforehand, but not more often than twice a day, for example, about midday and at night.

Reposition, moreover, may take place in a simpler way: the Priest or Deacon, wearing an alb, or a surplice over a cassock, and a stole, after a brief adoration and a prayer said with the faithful, replaces the Most Blessed Sacrament in the tabernacle. In the same way, at the appointed time, exposition may take place once more.[8]

---

[6] Cf. *ibidem*, no. 63: *loc. cit.*, p. 571.

[7] Cf. *ibidem*, no. 64: *loc. cit.*, p. 572.

[8] Cf. *ibidem*, no. 65: *loc. cit.*, p. 572.

Brief Expositions

89. Brief expositions of the Most Blessed Sacrament are to be arranged in such a way that, before benediction with the Most Blessed Sacrament, a suitable time is allowed for readings from the word of God, for hymns, prayers and a certain length of time for silent prayer.

Exposition which is held solely to impart benediction is prohibited.[9]

Adoration in Religious Communities

90. For religious communities and pious groups who, according to the customs or norms of their Institute, give their time to perpetual Eucharistic adoration, or adoration extended over a longer time, it is strongly recommended that they arrange this pious custom according to the spirit of the Sacred Liturgy, so that, when adoration of Christ the Lord takes place with the participation of the whole community, it may be carried out with sacred readings, song, and sacred silence, so that it may serve more effectively to nurture the spiritual life of the community. In this way, the spirit of unity and fraternity, which the Eucharist signifies and effects, will be promoted among the members of the religious house, and the worship offered to the Sacrament will be conducted in nobler manner.

Also to be observed, and highly commended, is that form of adoration in which one or two members of the community take turns before the Sacrament. Indeed, in this way, according to the rule of the Institute, approved by the Church, they adore and pray to Christ the Lord in the Sacrament, in the name of the whole community and of the Church.

III. The Minister of Exposition of the Most Holy Eucharist

91. The ordinary minister of the exposition of the Most Blessed Sacrament is a Priest or Deacon, who at the end of the adoration, before the Sacrament is reposed, blesses the people with the Sacrament itself.

In the absence of a Priest or Deacon, or if they are prevented by some good reason, the Most Holy Eucharist may be publicly exposed for the adoration of the faithful and then reposed by an acolyte or by another extraordinary minister of Holy Communion, or someone deputed by the local Ordinary.

---

[9] Cf. *ibidem*, no. 66: *loc. cit.*, p. 572.

All these may open the tabernacle and even, if it is appropriate, place the ciborium on the altar or place the host in a monstrance. At the end of the adoration they replace the Sacrament in the tabernacle. But it is not lawful for them to impart a blessing with the Most Blessed Sacrament.

92. The minister, if he is a Priest or Deacon, should wear an alb or a surplice over a cassock, and put on a white stole. In accordance with local custom, he may also wear a white cope.

Other ministers should put on either the liturgical vesture used in their region, or wear vesture that is not inappropriate for this ministry and has been approved by the Ordinary.

Furthermore, when imparting the blessing at the end of adoration, when the exposition takes place with a monstrance, both Priest and Deacon wear a white cope and humeral veil; if a ciborium is used, still they wear a humeral veil.

THE ORDER OF EUCHARISTIC EXPOSITION AND BENEDICTION

Exposition

93. When the people are gathered and, if appropriate, a liturgical song is being sung, the minister approaches the altar. If the Sacrament is not reserved at the altar where the exposition is to occur, the minister, after putting on a humeral veil, brings the Sacrament from the place of reservation, accompanied by servers or by the faithful with lighted candles.

The ciborium or monstrance should be placed upon the table of the altar covered with a cloth. If, however, exposition is extended over a longer period of time and takes place with a monstrance, a throne may be used, placed in a more prominent location; but care should be taken that it not be too elevated or distant.[10] When the exposition is completed, if the monstrance is used, the minister incenses the Sacrament. Meanwhile, in accordance with local custom, the following or another hymn or other Eucharistic song is sung:[10A]

[10]Cf. Sacred Congregation of Rites, Instruction *Eucharisticum mysterium*, no. 62: *Acta Apostolicæ Sedis* 59 (1967), p. 571.

[10A]Cf. below, nos. 192-199.

Or:

[Other melodies may be used.]

After this, if the adoration is extended over a longer period of time, he may withdraw.

94. If the exposition is more solemn and extended, the host to be used for adoration should be consecrated in the Mass that immediately precedes the exposition, and after Communion should be placed in the monstrance upon the altar. The Mass then should end with the Prayer after Communion, with the Concluding Rites omitted. Before the Priest leaves, however, he may place the Sacrament on the throne, if appropriate, and incense it, while, in accordance with local custom, O salutaris Hostia (O Victim bringing saving grace) (no. 93), or another hymn or other Eucharistic song is sung.

Adoration

95. During the exposition, prayers, liturgical songs, and readings should be so arranged that the faithful, attentive in prayer, may devote themselves to Christ the Lord.

To nourish personal prayer, there may be readings from Sacred Scripture with a homily or brief exhortation, which lead to a better appreciation of the Eucharistic Mystery. It is also fitting for the people to respond to the word of God by singing. It is desirable that a sacred silence occur at suitable times.

96. Some part of the Liturgy of the Hours, especially the principal hours, may also be celebrated in the presence of the Most Blessed Sacrament when it is exposed for a longer period. For through this liturgy, praise and thanksgiving, which are offered to God in the Eucharistic Celebration, are extended to the various hours of the day, and the supplications of the Church are directed to Christ and through him to the Father in the name of the whole world.

When Lauds (Morning Prayer) or Vespers (Evening Prayer) is celebrated during adoration, the conclusion **May the Lord bless us** is used, even by a Priest or Deacon. But when benediction follows immediately after any of the hours, the Concluding Prayer is said and the conclusion of the hour is omitted.

Benediction

97. Toward the end of adoration, the Priest or Deacon approaches the altar, genuflects and kneels, and the following or another hymn or other Eucharistic song is sung:[11]

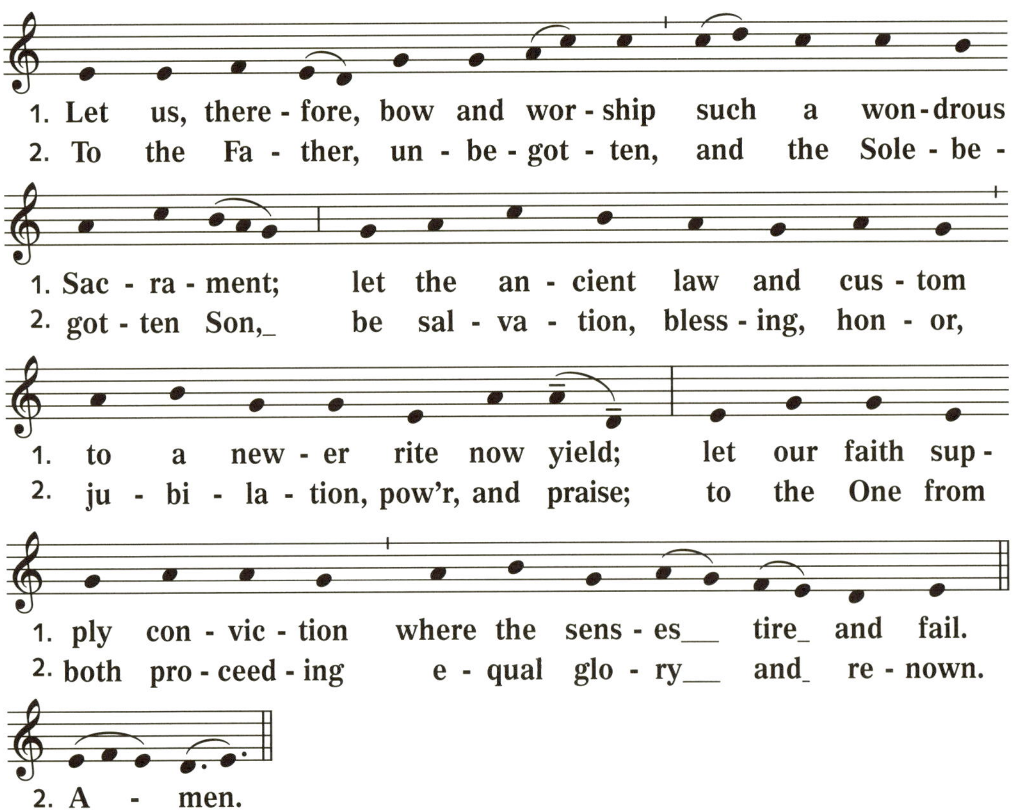

[11]Cf. below, nos. 192-199.

Or:

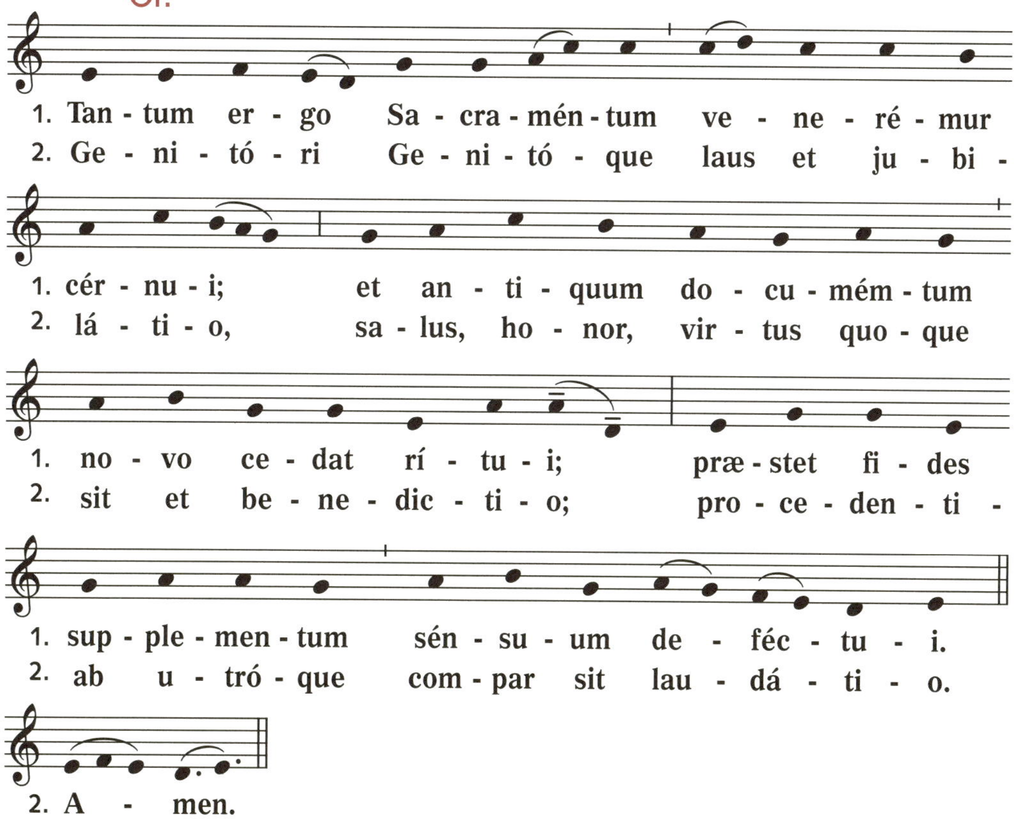

[Other melodies may be used.]

Meanwhile the minister, while kneeling, incenses the Most Blessed Sacrament if exposition has taken place with a monstrance.

98. After this the minister rises and says:

Let us pray.

A brief pause for silence follows. Then the minister continues:

O God, who in this wonderful Sacrament
have left us a memorial of your Passion,
grant us, we pray,
so to revere the sacred mysteries of your Body and Blood
that we may always experience in ourselves
the fruits of your redemption.
Who live and reign for ever and ever.

All reply:

Amen.

Other optional prayers, nos. 224-229.

99. Once the prayer has been said, the Priest or Deacon puts on a humeral veil, genuflects, and then takes the monstrance or ciborium and, with it, makes the Sign of the Cross over the people, without saying anything. A minister may incense the Most Blessed Sacrament, if appropriate, as the Priest or Deacon makes the Sign of the Cross with it over the people.

In accordance with local custom, the following acclamations may be sung or said in unison after the blessing with the Most Blessed Sacrament and before placing the Sacrament back in the tabernacle:

Blessed be God.
Blessed be his holy Name.
Blessed be Jesus Christ, true God and true man.
Blessed be the Name of Jesus.
Blessed be his most Sacred Heart.
Blessed be his most Precious Blood.
Blessed be Jesus in the most holy Sacrament of the altar.
Blessed be the Holy Spirit, the Paraclete.
Blessed be the great Mother of God, Mary most holy.
Blessed be her holy and Immaculate Conception.
Blessed be her glorious Assumption.
Blessed be the name of Mary, Virgin and Mother.
Blessed be Saint Joseph, her most chaste Spouse.
Blessed be God in his Angels and in his Saints.

Reposition

100. After the blessing, the Priest or Deacon who gave the blessing, or another Priest or Deacon, places the Sacrament back in the tabernacle and genuflects, while the people say an acclamation or sing a hymn, if appropriate. At the end, he leaves.

II. Eucharistic Processions

101. In processions in which the Eucharist is carried through the streets in a solemn rite with singing, the Christian people bear public witness of faith and devotion to the Most Blessed Sacrament.[12]

It is for the Diocesan Bishop, however, to judge concerning its appropriateness in the circumstances of today, and then concerning the time and place and arrangement of processions of this kind, so that they may be conducted with dignity and without harm to the reverence due to this Most Blessed Sacrament.

102. Among Eucharistic processions, the one that customarily takes place every year on the Solemnity of the Most Holy Body and Blood of Christ, or on another convenient day near to the Solemnity, holds particular importance and significance in the pastoral life of a parish or city. It is appropriate, therefore, when the circumstances of today permit and it can truly be a sign of common faith and adoration, that this procession be observed, in accordance with the law.

If, however, the city is very large and pastoral need suggests, it is lawful, at the discretion of the Diocesan Bishop, to arrange other processions in the principal districts of the city. But where it is not possible to hold a procession on the Solemnity of the Most Holy Body and Blood of Christ, it is fitting that another public celebration be held for the whole city, or for its principal districts, in the cathedral church or in other suitable places.

103. It is desirable that the procession with the Most Blessed Sacrament be held after the Mass in which the host to be carried in the procession has been consecrated. Nothing, however, prevents a procession being held even after an extended period of public adoration that follows Mass.

104. Eucharistic processions should be ordered in keeping with the customs of the place, with regard to the decoration of the public squares and streets, and in those things that pertain to the arrangement of the participants. While on the way, if the custom is in effect and pastoral advantage suggests, there may be stations where a Eucharistic blessing is given. Songs and prayers that are offered should be so ordered, that all may show their faith in Christ and direct their attention to the Lord alone.

105. The Priest who carries the Sacrament, if the procession occurs immediately after Mass, may continue to wear the sacred vestments used for the celebration of Mass, or he should put on a white cope. If, however, the procession does not immediately follow Mass, he wears a cope.

---

[12] Cf. Sacred Congregation of Rites, Instruction *Eucharisticum mysterium*, no. 59: *Acta Apostolicæ Sedis* 59 (1967), p. 570.

106. Lights, incense, and the canopy under which the Priest carrying the Sacrament walks should be used in accordance with local customs.

107. It is desirable that the procession should go from one church to another. Nevertheless, if local circumstances suggest it, the procession may also return to the same church from which it began.

108. At the end of the procession, benediction with the Most Blessed Sacrament is imparted in the church where the procession ends or at another more appropriate place. Then the Most Blessed Sacrament is reposed.

III. Eucharistic Congresses

109. Eucharistic congresses, which have been introduced into the life of the Church in more recent times as a special manifestation of Eucharistic worship, should be considered as a "station" to which a particular community invites the entire local Church, or a local Church invites other Churches of a particular region or nation, or even from the entire world, that together they may understand more deeply some aspect of the mystery of the Eucharist and worship it publicly in the bond of love and unity.

It is therefore essential that congresses of this sort be a true sign of faith and love by reason of the full participation of the local Church and the association, indicated above, of other Churches.

110. Suitable studies should be made of the place, theme and program for the celebration of the congresses, both by the local Church and by other Churches. These studies should lead to the consideration of genuine needs and should foster the progress of theological study and the good of the local Church. In these inquiries, the assistance of experts in theological, biblical, liturgical, and pastoral matters, as well as in the human sciences, should be employed.

111. In preparing for a congress, the following should be done above all:

a) more thorough catechesis on the Eucharist, especially as the mystery of Christ living and working in the Church, suited to the capacity of different groups;

b) more active participation in the Sacred Liturgy, fostering at the same time a prayerful hearing of the word of God and the fraternal sense of the community;[13]

[13]Second Vatican Council, Constitution on the Sacred Liturgy, *Sacrosanctum Concilium*, nos. 41-52; Dogmatic Constitution on the Church, *Lumen gentium*, no. 26.

c) the study of resources and the implementation of social works for the sake of human development and the right distribution of goods, including temporal goods, following the example of the primitive Christian community,[14] so that the leaven of the Gospel, as a force in the growth of contemporary society, and the pledge of future glory[15] may be diffused in some measure from the Eucharistic table.

112. The celebration itself of the congress should follow these criteria:[16]

a) the celebration of the Eucharist should truly be the center and summit to which all the undertakings and various forms of piety should be directed;

b) celebrations of the word of God, catechetical sessions, and public conferences should be planned, so that the proposed theme may be explored more deeply and its practical aspects set out more clearly;

c) opportunity should be given, either for common prayers or for extended adoration before the Most Blessed Sacrament, exposed in certain designated churches that seem more suitable for this pious exercise;

d) the norms for Eucharistic processions should be observed with regard to the organization of the procession, so that the Most Blessed Sacrament is carried through the streets of the city with common hymns and prayers,[17] taking into account the social and religious conditions of the place.

---

[14]Cf. Acts 4:32.

[15]Second Vatican Council, Constitution on the Sacred Liturgy, *Sacrosanctum Concilium*, no. 47; Decree on Ecumenism, *Unitatis redintegratio*, no. 15.

[16]Cf. Sacred Congregation of Rites, Instruction *Eucharisticum mysterium*, no. 67: *Acta Apostolicæ Sedis* 59 (1967), pp. 572-573.

[17]Cf. above, nos. 101-108.

A Ω

CHAPTER IV

VARIOUS TEXTS TO BE USED IN DISTRIBUTING HOLY COMMUNION OUTSIDE MASS AND IN THE ADORATION AND PROCESSION OF THE MOST BLESSED SACRAMENT

I. Biblical Readings

Readings from the Old Testament

Readings from the New Testament

Responsorial Psalms

Alleluia Verses and Verses before the Gospel

Gospel Readings

Readings from the Votive Mass of the Most Sacred Heart of Jesus

Readings from the Old Testament

Readings from the New Testament

Responsorial Psalms

Alleluia Verses and Verses before the Gospel

Gospel Readings

Readings from the Old Testament

(Lectionary for Mass, no. 976)

1 **113.** Genesis 14:18-20

Melchizedek brought out bread and wine.

A reading from the Book of Genesis

Melchizedek, king of Salem, brought out bread and wine,
and being a priest of God Most High,
he blessed Abram with these words:
"Blessed be Abram by God Most High,
the creator of heaven and earth;
And blessed be God Most High,
who delivered your foes into your hand."
Then Abram gave him a tenth of everything.

The word of the Lord.

2 114. Exodus 12:21-27

Seeing the blood on the lintel and the two doorposts,
the Lord will pass over that door.

A reading from the Book of Exodus

Moses called all the elders of the children of Israel and said to them,
"Go and procure lambs for your families,
and slaughter them as Passover victims.
Then take a bunch of hyssop,
and dipping it in the blood that is in the basin,
sprinkle the lintel and the two doorposts with this blood.
But none of you shall go outdoors until morning.
For the LORD will go by, striking down the Egyptians.
Seeing the blood on the lintel and the two doorposts,
the LORD will pass over that door
and not let the destroyer come into your houses to strike you down.

"You shall observe this as a perpetual ordinance
for yourselves and your descendants.
Thus, you must also observe this rite
when you have entered the land
which the LORD will give you as he promised.
When your children ask you,
'What does this rite of yours mean?' you shall reply,
'This is the Passover sacrifice of the LORD,
who passed over the houses of the children of Israel in Egypt;
when he struck down the Egyptians, he spared our houses.'"

Then the people bowed down in worship.

The word of the Lord.

3 **115.** Exodus 16:2-4, 12-15

I will now rain down bread from heaven for you.

A reading from the Book of Exodus

The whole congregation of the children of Israel
grumbled against Moses and Aaron.
The children of Israel said to them,
"Would that we had died at the LORD's hand in the land of Egypt,
as we sat by our fleshpots and ate our fill of bread!
But you had to lead us into this desert
to make the whole community die of famine!"

Then the LORD said to Moses,
"I will now rain down bread from heaven for you.
Each day the people are to go out and gather their daily portion;
thus will I test them,
to see whether they follow my instructions or not.

"I have heard the grumbling of the children of Israel.
Tell them: In the evening twilight you shall eat flesh,
and in the morning you shall have your fill of bread,
so that you may know that I, the LORD, am your God."

In the evening quail came up and covered the camp.
In the morning a dew lay all about the camp,
and when the dew evaporated, there on the surface of the desert
were fine flakes like hoarfrost on the ground.
On seeing it, the children of Israel asked one another, "What is this?"
for they did not know what it was.
But Moses told them,
"This is the bread that the LORD has given you to eat."

The word of the Lord.

4 116. Exodus 24:3-8

This is the blood of the covenant that the Lord has made with you.

A reading from the Book of Exodus

**When Moses came to the people
and related all the words and ordinances of the LORD,
they all answered with one voice,
"We will do everything that the LORD has told us."
Moses then wrote down all the words of the LORD and,
rising early the next day,
he erected at the foot of the mountain an altar
and twelve pillars for the twelve tribes of Israel.
Then, having sent certain young men of the children
of Israel
to offer burnt offerings and sacrifice young bulls
as peace offerings to the LORD,
Moses took half of the blood and put it in large bowls;
the other half he splashed on the altar.
Taking the book of the covenant, he read it aloud to
the people,
who answered, "All that the LORD has said, we will
heed and do."
Then he took the blood and sprinkled it on the people, saying,
"This is the blood of the covenant
that the LORD has made with you
in accordance with all these words of his."**

The word of the Lord.

5 117. Deuteronomy 8:2-3, 14b-16a

He fed you with manna, a food unknown to you and your fathers.

A reading from the Book of Deuteronomy

Moses said to the people:
"Remember how for forty years now the LORD,
your God,
has directed all your journeying in the desert,
so as to test you by affliction
and find out whether or not it was your intention
to keep his commandments.
He therefore let you be afflicted with hunger,
and then fed you with manna,
a food unknown to you and your fathers;
in order to show you that not by bread alone does one live,
but by every word that comes forth from the mouth of
the LORD.

"The LORD, your God,
who brought you out of the land of Egypt,
that place of slavery;
who guided you through the vast and terrible desert
with its saraph serpents and scorpions,
its parched and waterless ground;
who brought forth water for you from the flinty rock
and fed you in the desert with manna,
a food unknown to your fathers."

The word of the Lord.

6 118. 1 Kings 19:4-8

Strengthened by that food, he walked to the mountain of God.

A reading from the first Book of Kings

Elijah went a day's journey into the desert,
until he came to a broom tree and sat beneath it.
He prayed for death saying:
"This is enough, O LORD!
Take my life, for I am no better than my fathers."
He lay down and fell asleep under the broom tree,
but then an angel touched him and ordered him to get up and eat.
Elijah looked and there at his head was a hearth cake
and a jug of water.
After he ate and drank, he lay down again,
but the angel of the LORD came back a second time,
touched him, and ordered,
"Get up and eat, else the journey will be too long for you!"
He got up, ate, and drank;
then, strengthened by that food,
he walked forty days and forty nights to the mountain of God, Horeb.

The word of the Lord.

7 119. Proverbs 9:1-6

Come, eat of my food and drink of the wine I have mixed.

A reading from the Book of Proverbs

Wisdom has built her house,
she has set up her seven columns;
She has dressed her meat, mixed her wine,
yes, she has spread her table.
She has sent out her maidens; she calls
from the heights out over the city:
"Let whoever is simple turn in here;
to the one who lacks understanding, I say,

Come, eat of my food,
and drink of the wine I have mixed!
Forsake foolishness that you may live;
advance in the way of understanding."

The word of the Lord.

Readings from the New Testament

(*Lectionary for Mass*, nos. 977 and 979)

1 120. Acts of the Apostles 2:42-47

They devoted themselves to meeting together in the temple area and to breaking bread in their homes.

A reading from the Acts of the Apostles

The brothers and sisters devoted themselves
to the teaching of the Apostles and to the communal life,
to the breaking of the bread and to the prayers.
Awe came upon everyone,
and many wonders and signs were done through the Apostles.
All who believed were together and had all things in common;
they would sell their property and possessions
and divide them among all according to each one's need.
Every day they devoted themselves
to meeting together in the temple area
and to breaking bread in their homes.
They ate their meals with exultation and sincerity of heart,
praising God and enjoying favor with all the people.
And every day the Lord added to their number those who were being saved.

The word of the Lord.

2 121. Acts of the Apostles 10:34a, 37-43

We ate and drank with him after he rose from the dead.

A reading from the Acts of the Apostles

Peter proceeded to speak, saying:
"You know what has happened all over Judea,
beginning in Galilee after the baptism
that John preached,
how God anointed Jesus of Nazareth
with the Holy Spirit and power.
He went about doing good
and healing all those oppressed by the Devil,
for God was with him.
We are witnesses of all that he did
both in the country of the Jews and in Jerusalem.
They put him to death by hanging him on a tree.
This man God raised on the third day and granted that he be visible,
not to all the people, but to us,
the witnesses chosen by God in advance,
who ate and drank with him after he rose from the dead.
He commissioned us to preach to the people
and testify that he is the one appointed by God
as judge of the living and the dead.
To him all the prophets bear witness,
that everyone who believes in him
will receive forgiveness of sins through his name."

The word of the Lord.

3 122. 1 Corinthians 10:16-17

We, though many, are one bread, one Body.

A reading from the first Letter of Saint Paul to the Corinthians

Brothers and sisters:
The cup of blessing that we bless,
is it not a participation in the Blood of Christ?
The bread that we break,
is it not a participation in the Body of Christ?
Because the loaf of bread is one,
we, though many, are one Body,
for we all partake of the one loaf.

The word of the Lord.

4 123. 1 Corinthians 11:23-26

For as often as you eat the bread and drink the cup,
you proclaim the death of the Lord.

A reading from the first Letter of Saint Paul to the Corinthians

Brothers and sisters:
I received from the Lord what I also handed on to you,
that the Lord Jesus, on the night he was handed over,
took bread and, after he had given thanks,
broke it and said, "This is my Body that is for you.
Do this in remembrance of me."
In the same way also the cup, after supper, saying,
"This cup is the new covenant in my Blood.
Do this, as often as you drink it, in remembrance of me."
For as often as you eat this bread and drink the cup,
you proclaim the death of the Lord until he comes.

The word of the Lord.

5 **124.** Hebrews 9:11-15

The Blood of Christ will cleanse our consciences.

A reading from the Letter to the Hebrews

When Christ came as high priest
of the good things that have come to be,
passing through the greater and more perfect tabernacle
not made by hands, that is, not belonging to this creation,
he entered once for all into the sanctuary,
not with the blood of goats and calves
but with his own Blood, thus obtaining eternal redemption.
For if the blood of goats and bulls
and the sprinkling of a heifer's ashes
can sanctify those who are defiled
so that their flesh is cleansed,
how much more will the Blood of Christ,
who through the eternal Spirit offered himself unblemished to God,
cleanse our consciences from dead works to worship the living God.

For this reason he is mediator of a new covenant:
since a death has taken place for deliverance from transgressions
under the first covenant,
those who are called may receive the promised eternal inheritance.

The word of the Lord.

6 125. Hebrews 12:18-19, 22-24

You have approached the sprinkled Blood that speaks more eloquently than that of Abel.

A reading from the Letter to the Hebrews

Brothers and sisters:
You have not approached that which could be touched
and a blazing fire and gloomy darkness
and storm and a trumpet blast
and a voice speaking words such that those who heard
begged that no message be further addressed to them.
No, you have approached Mount Zion
and the city of the living God, the heavenly Jerusalem,
and countless angels in festal gathering,
and the assembly of the firstborn enrolled in heaven,
and God the judge of all,
and the spirits of the just made perfect,
and Jesus, the mediator of a new covenant,
and the sprinkled Blood that speaks more eloquently
than that of Abel.

The word of the Lord.

7 126. 1 Peter 1:17-21

You were ransomed with the precious Blood of Christ, as of a spotless unblemished Lamb.

A reading from the first Letter of Saint Peter

Beloved:
If you invoke as Father him who judges impartially
according to each one's works,
conduct yourselves with reverence during the time of your sojourning,
realizing that you were ransomed from your futile conduct,
handed on by your ancestors,

not with perishable things like silver or gold
but with the precious Blood of Christ
as of a spotless unblemished Lamb.
He was known before the foundation of the world
but revealed in the final time for you,
who through him believe in God
who raised him from the dead and gave him glory,
so that your faith and hope are in God.

The word of the Lord.

8 127. 1 John 5:4-8

So there are three that testify, the Spirit, the water, and the Blood.

A reading from the first Letter of Saint John

Beloved:
Whoever is begotten by God conquers the world.
And the victory that conquers the world is our faith.
Who indeed is the victor over the world
but the one who believes that Jesus is the Son of God?

This is the one who came through water and Blood,
Jesus Christ,
not by water alone, but by water and Blood.
The Spirit is the one that testifies,
and the Spirit is truth.
So there are three that testify,
the Spirit, the water, and the Blood,
and the three are of one accord.

The word of the Lord.

9 **128.** Revelation 1:5-8

To him who loves us and freed us from our sins by his Blood.

A reading from the Book of Revelation

Grace to you and peace from Jesus Christ, who is the faithful witness,
the firstborn of the dead and ruler of the kings of the earth.
To him who loves us and has freed us from our sins by his Blood,
who has made us into a kingdom, priests for his God and Father,
to him be glory and power forever and ever. Amen.

Behold, he is coming amid the clouds,
and every eye will see him,
even those who pierced him.
All the peoples of the earth will lament him.
Yes. Amen.
"I am the Alpha and the Omega," says the Lord God,
"the one who is and who was and who is to come, the almighty."

The word of the Lord.

10 **129.** Revelation 7:9-14

They have washed their robes and made them white in the Blood of the Lamb.

A reading from the Book of Revelation

I, John, had a vision of a great multitude,
which no one could count,
from every nation, race, people, and tongue.
They stood before the throne and before the Lamb,
wearing white robes and holding palm branches in their hands.
They cried out in a loud voice:

"Salvation comes from our God, who is seated on the throne,
and from the Lamb."

All the angels stood around the throne
and around the elders and the four living creatures.
They prostrated themselves before the throne,
worshiped God, and exclaimed:

"Amen. Blessing and glory, wisdom and thanksgiving,
honor, power, and might
be to our God forever and ever. Amen."

Then one of the elders spoke up and said to me,
"Who are these wearing white robes, and where did they come from?"
I said to him,"My lord, you are the one who knows."
He said to me,
"These are the ones who have survived the time of great distress;
they have washed their robes
and made them white in the Blood of the Lamb."

The word of the Lord.

Responsorial Psalms

(*Lectionary for Mass*, no. 978)

1 **130.** Psalm 23 (22):1-3, 4, 5, 6

℟. (1) The Lord is my shepherd; there is nothing I shall want.

Or:

℟. Alleluia.

The Lord is my shepherd;
there is nothing I shall want.
Fresh and green are the pastures
where he gives me repose.
Near restful waters he leads me;
he revives my soul.
He guides me along the right path,
for the sake of his name.

℟. The Lord is my shepherd; there is nothing I shall want.

Or:

℟. Alleluia.

Though I should walk in the valley of the shadow of death,
no evil would I fear, for you are with me.
Your crook and your staff will give me comfort.

℟. The Lord is my shepherd; there is nothing I shall want.

Or:

℟. Alleluia.

You have prepared a table before me
in the sight of my foes.
My head you have anointed with oil;
my cup is overflowing.

℟. The Lord is my shepherd; there is nothing I shall want.

Or:

℟. Alleluia.

Surely goodness and mercy shall follow me
all the days of my life.
In the LORD's own house shall I dwell
for length of days unending.

℟. The Lord is my shepherd; there is nothing I shall want.

Or:

℟. Alleluia.

2 131. Psalm 34 (33):2-3, 4-5, 6-7, 8-9, 10-11

℟. (9a) Taste and see that the Lord is good.

Or:

℟. Alleluia.

I will bless the LORD at all times,
praise of him is always in my mouth.
In the LORD my soul shall make its boast;
the humble shall hear and be glad.

℟. Taste and see that the Lord is good.

Or:

℟. Alleluia.

Glorify the LORD with me;
together let us praise his name.
I sought the LORD, and he answered me;
from all my terrors he set me free.

℟. Taste and see that the Lord is good.

Or:

℟. Alleluia.

Look toward him and be radiant;
let your faces not be abashed.
This lowly one called; the LORD heard,
and rescued him from all his distress.

℟. Taste and see that the Lord is good.

Or:

℟. Alleluia.

The angel of the LORD is encamped
around those who fear him, to rescue them.
Taste and see that the LORD is good.
Blessed the man who seeks refuge in him.

℟. Taste and see that the Lord is good.

Or:

℟. Alleluia.

Fear the LORD, you his holy ones.
They lack nothing, those who fear him.
The rich suffer want and go hungry,
but those who seek the LORD lack no blessing.

℟. Taste and see that the Lord is good.

Or:

℟. Alleluia.

3 **132.** Psalm 40 (39):2 and 4ab, 7-8a, 8b-9, 10

℟. (8a, 9a) Behold, O Lord, I have come to do your will.

I waited, I waited for the Lord,
and he stooped down to me;
he heard my cry.
He put a new song into my mouth,
praise of our God.

℟. Behold, O Lord, I have come to do your will.

You delight not in sacrifice and offering,
but in an open ear.
You do not ask for holocaust and sin offering.
Then I said, "Behold, I have come."

℟. Behold, O Lord, I have come to do your will.

In the scroll of the book it stands written of me:
"I delight to do your will, O my God;
your instruction lies deep within me."

℟. Behold, O Lord, I have come to do your will.

Your uprightness I have proclaimed
in the great assembly.
My lips I have not sealed;
you know it, O Lord.

℟. Behold, O Lord, I have come to do your will.

4 **133.** Psalm 78 (77):3-4a and 7ab, 23-24, 25 and 54

℟. (24b) The Lord gave them bread from heaven.

The things we have heard and understood,
the things our fathers have told us,
these we will not hide from their children:
that they should set their hope in God,
and never forget God's deeds.

℟. The Lord gave them bread from heaven.

He commanded the clouds above,
and opened the gates of heaven.
He rained down manna to eat,
and gave them bread from heaven.

℟. The Lord gave them bread from heaven.

Man ate the bread of angels.
He sent them abundance of food.
He brought them to his holy land,
to the mountain his right hand had won.

℟. The Lord gave them bread from heaven.

5 134. Psalm 110 (109):1, 2, 3, 4

℟. (4bc) You are a priest forever, according to the order of Melchizedek.

Or:

℟. Christ the Lord, a priest for ever in the line of Melchizedek, offered bread and wine.

The LORD's revelation to my lord:
"Sit at my right hand,
until I make your foes your footstool."

℟. You are a priest forever, according to the order of Melchizedek.

Or:

℟. Christ the Lord, a priest for ever in the line of Melchizedek, offered bread and wine.

The LORD will send from Zion
your scepter of power:
rule in the midst of your foes.

℟. You are a priest forever, according to the order of Melchizedek.

Or:

℟. Christ the Lord, a priest for ever in the line of Melchizedek, offered bread and wine.

With you is princely rule
on the day of your power.
In holy splendor, from the womb before the dawn,
I have begotten you.

℟. You are a priest forever, according to the order of Melchizedek.

Or:

℟. Christ the Lord, a priest for ever in the line of Melchizedek, offered bread and wine.

The Lord has sworn an oath he will not change:
"You are a priest forever,
according to the order of Melchizedek."

℟. You are a priest forever, according to the order of Melchizedek.

Or:

℟. Christ the Lord, a priest for ever in the line of Melchizedek, offered bread and wine.

6 **135.** Psalm 116 (115):12-13, 15-16, 17-18

℟. (13) The cup of salvation I will raise; I will call on the name of the Lord.

Or:

℟. (1 Corinthians 10:16) Our blessing-cup is a communion with the Blood of Christ.

Or:

℟. Alleluia.

How can I repay the Lord
for all his goodness to me?
The cup of salvation I will raise;
I will call on the name of the Lord.

℟. The cup of salvation I will raise; I will call on the name of the Lord.

Or:

℟. Our blessing-cup is a communion with the Blood of Christ.

Or:

℟. Alleluia.

How precious in the eyes of the LORD
is the death of his faithful.
Your servant, LORD, your servant am I,
the son of your handmaid;
you have loosened my bonds.

℟. The cup of salvation I will raise; I will call on the name of the Lord.

Or:

℟. Our blessing-cup is a communion with the Blood of Christ.

Or:

℟. Alleluia.

I will offer you a thanksgiving sacrifice;
I will call on the name of the LORD.
My vows to the LORD I will fulfill
before all his people.

℟. The cup of salvation I will raise; I will call on the name of the Lord.

Or:

℟. Our blessing-cup is a communion with the Blood of Christ.

Or:

℟. Alleluia.

7 136. Psalm 145 (144):10-11, 15-16, 17-18

℟. (cf. 16) Lord, you open your hand and feed us.

All your works shall thank you, O LORD,
and all your faithful ones bless you.
They shall speak of the glory of your reign,
and declare your mighty deeds.

℟. Lord, you open your hand and feed us.

The eyes of all look to you,
and you give them their food in due season.
You open your hand and satisfy
the desire of every living thing.

℟. Lord, you open your hand and feed us.

The LORD is just in all his ways,
and holy in all his deeds.
The LORD is close to all who call him,
who call on him in truth.

℟. Lord, you open your hand and feed us.

8 137. Psalm 147:12-13, 14-15, 19-20

℟. (12a) O Jerusalem, glorify the Lord!

Or:

℟. (John 6:58c) Whoever eats this bread will live for ever.

Or:

℟. Alleluia.

O Jerusalem, glorify the LORD!
O Zion, praise your God!
He has strengthened the bars of your gates;
he has blessed your children within you.

℟. O Jerusalem, glorify the Lord!

Or:

℟. Whoever eats this bread will live for ever.

Or:

℟. Alleluia.

He established peace on your borders;
he gives you your fill of finest wheat.
He sends out his word to the earth,
and swiftly runs his command.

℟. O Jerusalem, glorify the Lord!

Or:

℟. Whoever eats this bread will live for ever.

Or:

℟. Alleluia.

He reveals his word to Jacob;
to Israel, his decrees and judgments.
He has not dealt thus with other nations;
he has not taught them his judgments.

℟. O Jerusalem, glorify the Lord!

Or:

℟. Whoever eats this bread will live for ever.

Or:

℟. Alleluia.

Alleluia Verses and Verses before the Gospel

(*Lectionary for Mass*, no. 980)

1 138. John 6:51

**I am the living bread that came down from heaven,
says the Lord;
whoever eats this bread will live forever.**

2 139. John 6:56

**Whoever eats my Flesh and drinks my Blood
remains in me, and I in him, says the Lord.**

3 140. John 6:57

**Just as the living Father sent me and I have life because of the Father,
so also the one who feeds on me will have life because of me.**

4 141. Cf. Revelation 1:5ab

**Jesus Christ, you are the faithful witness,
the firstborn of the dead,
you have loved us and freed us from our sins by your Blood.**

5 142. Revelation 5:9

**Worthy are you, O Lord, to receive the scroll and to break open its seals,
for you were slain and with your Blood you have ransomed us for God.**

Gospel Readings

(Lectionary for Mass, no. 981)

1 143. Mark 14:12-16, 22-26

This is my Body. This is my Blood.

✠ **A reading from the holy Gospel according to Mark**

On the first day of the Feast of Unleavened Bread,
when they sacrificed the Passover Lamb,
the disciples of Jesus said to him,
"Where do you want us to go
and prepare for you to eat the Passover?"
He sent two of his disciples and said to them,
"Go into the city and a man will meet you,
carrying a jar of water.
Follow him.
Wherever he enters, say to the master of the house,
'The Teacher says, "Where is my guest room
where I may eat the Passover with my disciples?"'
Then he will show you a large upper room furnished and ready.
Make the preparations for us there."
The disciples then went off, entered the city,
and found it just as he had told them;
and they prepared the Passover.

While they were eating,
he took bread, said the blessing,
broke it, gave it to them, and said,
"Take it; this is my Body."
Then he took a cup, gave thanks, and gave it to them,
and they all drank from it.
He said to them,
"This is my Blood of the covenant,
which will be shed for many.
Amen, I say to you,

I shall not drink again the fruit of the vine
until the day when I drink it new in the Kingdom of God."
Then, after singing a hymn,
they went out to the Mount of Olives.

The Gospel of the Lord.

2 144. Mark 15:16-20

They clothed him in purple and, weaving a crown of thorns, placed it on him.

✠ A reading from the holy Gospel according to Mark

The soldiers led Jesus away inside the palace,
that is, the praetorium, and assembled the whole cohort.
They clothed him in purple and,
weaving a crown of thorns, placed it on him.
They began to salute him with,"Hail, King of the Jews!"
and kept striking his head with a reed and spitting upon him.
They knelt before him in homage.
And when they had mocked him,
they stripped him of the purple cloak,
dressed him in his own clothes,
and led him out to crucify him.

The Gospel of the Lord.

3 145. Luke 9:11b-17

They all ate and were satisfied.

✠ **A reading from the holy Gospel according to Luke**

**Jesus spoke to the crowds about the Kingdom of God,
and he healed those who needed to be cured.
As the day was drawing to a close,
the Twelve approached him and said,
"Dismiss the crowd
so that they can go to the surrounding villages and farms
and find lodging and provisions;
for we are in a deserted place here."
He said to them, "Give them some food yourselves."
They replied, "Five loaves and two fish are all we have,
unless we ourselves go and buy food for all these people."
Now the men there numbered about five thousand.
Then he said to his disciples,
"Have them sit down in groups of about fifty."
They did so and made them all sit down.
Then taking the five loaves and the two fish,
and looking up to heaven,
he said the blessing over them, broke them,
and gave them to the disciples to set before the crowd.
They all ate and were satisfied.
And when the leftover fragments were picked up,
they filled twelve wicker baskets.**

The Gospel of the Lord.

4 146. Luke 22:39-44

His sweat became like drops of blood, falling on the ground.

✠ A reading from the holy Gospel according to Luke

Jesus went, as was his custom, to the Mount of Olives,
and the disciples followed him.
When he arrived at the place he said to them,
"Pray that you may not undergo the test."
After withdrawing about a stone's throw from them
and kneeling,
Jesus prayed, saying, "Father, if you are willing,
take this cup away from me;
still, not my will but yours be done."
And to strengthen him an angel from heaven appeared
to him.
He was in such agony and he prayed so fervently
that his sweat became like drops of blood
falling on the ground.

The Gospel of the Lord.

5 147. Luke 24:13-35

They recognized him in the breaking of bread.

(LONG FORM)

✠ A reading from the holy Gospel according to Luke

That very day, the first day of the week,
two of the disciples of Jesus were going
to a village called Emmaus, seven miles from Jerusalem,
and they were conversing about all the things that
had occurred.
And it happened that while they were conversing
and debating,

Jesus himself drew near and walked with them,
but their eyes were prevented from recognizing him.
He asked them,
"What are you discussing as you walk along?"
They stopped, looking downcast.
One of them, named Cleopas, said to him in reply,
"Are you the only visitor to Jerusalem
who does not know of the things
that have taken place there in these days?"
And he replied to them, "What sort of things?"
They said to him,
"The things that happened to Jesus the Nazarene,
who was a prophet mighty in deed and word
before God and all the people,
how our chief priests and rulers both handed him over
to a sentence of death and crucified him.
But we were hoping that he would be the one to redeem Israel;
and besides all this,
it is now the third day since this took place.
Some women from our group, however, have astounded us:
they were at the tomb early in the morning
and did not find his Body;
they came back and reported
that they had indeed seen a vision of angels
who announced that he was alive.
Then some of those with us went to the tomb
and found things just as the women had described,
but him they did not see."
And he said to them, "Oh, how foolish you are!
How slow of heart to believe all that the prophets spoke!
Was it not necessary that the Christ should suffer
these things
and enter into his glory?"
Then beginning with Moses and all the prophets,
he interpreted to them what referred to him
in all the Scriptures.

As they approached the village to which they were going,
he gave the impression that he was going on farther.
But they urged him, "Stay with us,
for it is nearly evening and the day is almost over."
So he went in to stay with them.
And it happened that, while he was with them at table,
he took bread, said the blessing,
broke it, and gave it to them.
With that their eyes were opened and they recognized him,
but he vanished from their sight.
Then they said to each other,
"Were not our hearts burning within us
while he spoke to us on the way and opened the Scriptures to us?"
So they set out at once and returned to Jerusalem
where they found gathered together
the Eleven and those with them, who were saying,
"The Lord has truly been raised and has appeared to Simon!"
Then the two recounted
what had taken place on the way
and how he was made known to them in the breaking of bread.

The Gospel of the Lord.

Or:

Luke 24:13-16, 28-35

(SHORT FORM)

✠ A reading from the holy Gospel according to Luke

That very day, the first day of the week,
two of the disciples of Jesus were going
to a village called Emmaus, seven miles from Jerusalem,

and they were conversing about all the things that had occurred.
And it happened that while they were conversing and debating,
Jesus himself drew near and walked with them,
but their eyes were prevented from recognizing him.
As they approached the village to which they were going,
he gave the impression that he was going on farther.
But they urged him, "Stay with us,
for it is nearly evening and the day is almost over."
So he went in to stay with them.
And it happened that, while he was with them at table,
he took bread, said the blessing,
broke it, and gave it to them.
With that their eyes were opened and they recognized him,
but he vanished from their sight.
Then they said to each other,
"Were not our hearts burning within us
while he spoke to us on the way and opened the Scriptures to us?"
So they set out at once and returned to Jerusalem
where they found gathered together
the Eleven and those with them, who were saying,
"The Lord has truly been raised and has appeared to Simon!"
Then the two recounted
what had taken place on the way
and how he was made known to them in the breaking of bread.

The Gospel of the Lord.

6 148. John 6:1-15

He distributed to those who were reclining as much as they wanted.

✠ **A reading from the holy Gospel according to John**

Jesus went across the Sea of Galilee.
A large crowd followed him,
because they saw the signs he was performing on the sick.
Jesus went up on the mountain,
and there he sat down with his disciples.
The Jewish feast of Passover was near.
When Jesus raised his eyes
and saw that a large crowd was coming to him,
he said to Philip,
"Where can we buy enough food for them to eat?"
He said this to test him,
because he himself knew what he was going to do.
Philip answered him,
"Two hundred days' wages worth of food would not be enough
for each of them to have a little."
One of his disciples,
Andrew, the brother of Simon Peter, said to him,
"There is a boy here who has five barley loaves and two fish;
but what good are these for so many?"
Jesus said, "Have the people recline."
Now there was a great deal of grass in that place.
So the men reclined, about five thousand in number.
Then Jesus took the loaves, gave thanks,
and distributed them to those who were reclining,
and also as much of the fish as they wanted.

When they had had their fill, he said to his disciples,
"Gather the fragments left over,
so that nothing will be wasted."
So they collected them,
and filled twelve wicker baskets with fragments
from the five barley loaves that had been more than they could eat.
When the people saw the sign he had done, they said,
"This is truly the prophet, the one who is to come into the world."
Since Jesus knew that they were going to come
and carry him off to make him king,
he withdrew again to the mountain alone.

The Gospel of the Lord.

7

149. John 6:24-35

*Whoever comes to me will never hunger,
and whoever believes in me will never thirst.*

✠ **A reading from the holy Gospel according to John**

**When the crowd saw that neither Jesus nor his disciples were there,
they themselves got into boats
and came to Capernaum looking for Jesus.
And when they found him across the sea they said to him,
"Rabbi, when did you get here?"
Jesus answered them and said,
"Amen, amen, I say to you,
you are looking for me not because you saw signs
but because you ate the loaves and were filled.
Do not work for food that perishes
but for the food that endures for eternal life,
which the Son of Man will give you.
For on him the Father, God, has set his seal."
So they said to him,
"What can we do to accomplish the works of God?"
Jesus answered and said to them,
"This is the work of God, that you believe in the one he sent."
So they said to him,
"What sign can you do, that we may see and believe in you?
What can you do?
Our ancestors ate manna in the desert, as it is written:
He gave them bread from heaven to eat."
So Jesus said to them,
"Amen, amen, I say to you,
it was not Moses who gave the bread from heaven;
my Father gives you the true bread from heaven.**

For the bread of God is that which comes down from heaven
and gives life to the world."
So they said to him,
"Sir, give us this bread always."
Jesus said to them,
"I am the bread of life;
whoever comes to me will never hunger,
and whoever believes in me will never thirst."

The Gospel of the Lord.

8 150. John 6:41-51

I am the living bread that came down from heaven.

✠ **A reading from the holy Gospel according to John**

The Jews murmured about Jesus because he said,
"I am the bread that came down from heaven,"
and they said,
"Is this not Jesus, the son of Joseph?
Do we not know his father and mother?
Then how can he say,
'I have come down from heaven'?"
Jesus answered and said to them,
"Stop murmuring among yourselves.
No one can come to me unless the Father who sent me draw him,
and I will raise him on the last day.
It is written in the prophets:
They shall all be taught by God.
Everyone who listens to my Father and learns from him comes to me.
Not that anyone has seen the Father
except the one who is from God;
he has seen the Father.
Amen, amen, I say to you,
whoever believes has eternal life.
I am the bread of life.
Your ancestors ate the manna in the desert, but they died;
this is the bread that comes down from heaven
so that one may eat it and not die.
I am the living bread that came down from heaven;
whoever eats this bread will live forever;
and the bread that I will give
is my Flesh for the life of the world."

The Gospel of the Lord.

9

151. John 6:51-58

My Flesh is true food and my Blood is true drink.

✠ **A reading from the holy Gospel according to John**

Jesus said to the Jews who were present:
"I am the living bread that came down from heaven;
whoever eats this bread will live forever;
and the bread that I will give
is my Flesh for the life of the world."

The Jews quarreled among themselves, saying,
"How can this man give us his Flesh to eat?"
Jesus said to them,
"Amen, amen, I say to you,
unless you eat the Flesh of the Son of Man and drink his Blood,
you do not have life within you.
Whoever eats my Flesh and drinks my Blood
has eternal life,
and I will raise him on the last day.
For my Flesh is true food,
and my Blood is true drink.
Whoever eats my Flesh and drinks my Blood
remains in me and I in him.
Just as the living Father sent me
and I have life because of the Father,
so also the one who feeds on me
will have life because of me.
This is the bread that came down from heaven.
Unlike your ancestors who ate and still died,
whoever eats this bread will live forever."

The Gospel of the Lord.

10 **152.** John 19:31-37

One soldier thrust his lance into his side and immediately Blood and water flowed out.

✠ **A reading from the holy Gospel according to John**

Since it was preparation day,
in order that the bodies might not remain on the cross on the sabbath,
for the sabbath day of that week was a solemn one,
the Jews asked Pilate that their legs be broken
and they be taken down.
So the soldiers came and broke the legs of the first
and then of the other one who was crucified with Jesus.
But when they came to Jesus and saw that he was already dead,
they did not break his legs,
but one soldier thrust his lance into his side,
and immediately Blood and water flowed out.
An eyewitness has testified, and his testimony is true;
he knows that he is speaking the truth,
so that you also may come to believe.
For this happened so that the Scripture passage might be fulfilled:
Not a bone of it will be broken.
And again another passage says:
They will look upon him whom they have pierced.

The Gospel of the Lord.

11 153. John 21:1-14

Jesus came over and took the bread and gave it to them.

✠ A reading from the holy Gospel according to John

Jesus revealed himself again to his disciples at the Sea of Tiberias.
He revealed himself in this way.
Together were Simon Peter, Thomas called Didymus,
Nathanael from Cana in Galilee,
Zebedee's sons, and two others of his disciples.
Simon Peter said to them, "I am going fishing."
They said to him, "We also will come with you."
So they went out and got into the boat,
but that night they caught nothing.
When it was already dawn, Jesus was standing on the shore;
but the disciples did not realize that it was Jesus.
Jesus said to them, "Children, have you caught anything to eat?"
They answered him, "No."
So he said to them, "Cast the net over the right side of the boat
and you will find something."
So they cast it, and were not able to pull it in
because of the number of fish.
So the disciple whom Jesus loved said to Peter, "It is the Lord."
When Simon Peter heard that it was the Lord,
he tucked in his garment, for he was lightly clad,
and jumped into the sea.
The other disciples came in the boat,
for they were not far from shore, only about a hundred yards,
dragging the net with the fish.
When they climbed out on shore,
they saw a charcoal fire with fish on it and bread.

Jesus said to them, "Bring some of the fish you just caught."
So Simon Peter went over and dragged the net ashore
full of one hundred fifty-three large fish.
Even though there were so many, the net was not torn.
Jesus said to them, "Come, have breakfast."
And none of the disciples dared to ask him, "Who are you?"
because they realized it was the Lord.
Jesus came over and took the bread and gave it to them,
and in like manner the fish.
This was now the third time Jesus was revealed to
his disciples
after being raised from the dead.

The Gospel of the Lord.

READINGS FROM THE VOTIVE MASS OF THE MOST SACRED HEART OF JESUS

Readings from the Old Testament

(Lectionary for Mass, no. 995)

1 154. Exodus 34:4b-6, 8-9

The Lord, the Lord, a merciful and gracious God.

A reading from the Book of Exodus

Early in the morning Moses went up Mount Sinai
as the Lord had commanded him,
taking along the two stone tablets.

Having come down in a cloud, the Lord stood with Moses there
and proclaimed his name, "Lord."
Thus the Lord passed before him and cried out,
"The Lord, the Lord, a merciful and gracious God,
slow to anger and rich in kindness and fidelity."
Moses at once bowed down to the ground in worship.
Then he said, "If I find favor with you, O Lord,
do come along in our company.
This is indeed a stiff-necked people; yet pardon our wickedness and sins,
and receive us as your own."

The word of the Lord.

2 155. Deuteronomy 7:6-11

The Lord set his heart on you and chose you.

A reading from the Book of Deuteronomy

Moses said to the people:
"You are a people sacred to the Lord, your God;
he has chosen you from all the nations on the face of the earth
to be a people peculiarly his own.

It was not because you are the largest of all nations
that the LORD set his heart on you and chose you,
for you are really the smallest of all nations.
It was because the LORD loved you
and because of his fidelity to the oath he had sworn to your fathers,
that he brought you out with his strong hand
from the place of slavery,
and ransomed you from the hand of Pharaoh, king of Egypt.
Understand, then, that the LORD, your God, is God indeed,
the faithful God who keeps his merciful covenant
down to the thousandth generation
toward those who love him and keep his commandments,
but who repays with destruction the person who hates him;
he does not dally with such a one,
but makes him personally pay for it.
You shall therefore carefully observe the commandments,
the statutes, and the decrees which I enjoin on you today."

The word of the Lord.

3 156. Deuteronomy 10:12-22

Yet in his love for your fathers,
the Lord chose you, their descendants.

A reading from the Book of Deuteronomy

Moses said to the people:
"And now, Israel, what does the LORD, your God, ask of you
but to fear the LORD, your God, and follow his ways exactly,
to love and serve the LORD, your God,

with all your heart and all your soul,
to keep the commandments and statutes of the LORD
which I enjoin on you today for your own good?
Think! The heavens, even the highest heavens,
belong to the LORD, your God,
as well as the earth and everything on it.
Yet in his love for your fathers the LORD was so attached to them
as to choose you, their descendants,
in preference to all other peoples, as indeed he has now done.
Circumcise your hearts, therefore, and be no longer stiff-necked.
For the LORD, your God, is the God of gods,
the LORD of lords, the great God, mighty and awesome,
who has no favorites, accepts no bribes;
who executes justice for the orphan and the widow,
and befriends the alien, feeding and clothing them.
So you too must befriend the alien,
for you were once aliens yourselves in the land of Egypt.
The LORD, your God, shall you fear, and him shall you serve;
hold fast to him and swear by his name.
He is your glory, he, your God,
who has done for you those great and terrible things
which your own eyes have seen.
Your ancestors went down to Egypt seventy strong,
and now the LORD, your God,
has made you as numerous as the stars of the sky."

The word of the Lord.

4 157. Isaiah 49:13-15

Even if she should forget, I will never forget you.

A reading from the Book of the Prophet Isaiah

Sing out, O heavens, and rejoice, O earth,
break forth into song, you mountains.
For the LORD comforts his people
and shows mercy to his afflicted.

But Zion said, "The LORD has forsaken me;
my Lord has forgotten me."
Can a mother forget her infant,
be without tenderness for the child of her womb?
Even should she forget,
I will never forget you.

The word of the Lord.

5 158. Jeremiah 31:1-4

With an age-old love I have loved you.

A reading from the Book of the Prophet Jeremiah

At that time, says the LORD,
I will be the God of all the tribes of Israel,
and they shall be my people.
Thus says the LORD:
The people that escaped the sword
have found favor in the desert.
As Israel comes forward to be given his rest,
the LORD appears to him from afar:
With age-old love I have loved you;
so I have kept my mercy toward you.
Again I will restore you, and you shall be rebuilt,
O virgin Israel;
Carrying your festive tambourines,
you shall go forth dancing with the merrymakers.

The word of the Lord.

6 159. Ezekiel 34:11-16

I myself will look after and tend my sheep.

A reading from the Book of the Prophet Ezekiel

Thus says the Lord God:
I myself will look after and tend my sheep.
As a shepherd tends his flock
when he finds himself among his scattered sheep,
so will I tend my sheep.
I will rescue them from every place where they were scattered
when it was cloudy and dark.
I will lead them out from among the peoples
and gather them from the foreign lands;
I will bring them back to their own country
and pasture them upon the mountains of Israel
in the land's ravines and all its inhabited places.
In good pastures will I pasture them,
and on the mountain heights of Israel
shall be their grazing ground.
There they shall lie down on good grazing ground,
and in rich pastures shall they be pastured
on the mountains of Israel.
I myself will pasture my sheep;
I myself will give them rest, says the Lord God.
The lost I will seek out,
the strayed I will bring back,
the injured I will bind up,
the sick I will heal,
but the sleek and the strong I will destroy,
shepherding them rightly.

The word of the Lord.

7 **160.** Hosea 11:1, 3-4, 8c-9

My heart is overwhelmed.

A reading from the Book of the Prophet Hosea

Thus says the LORD:
When Israel was a child I loved him,
out of Egypt I called my son.
Yet it was I who taught Ephraim to walk,
who took them in my arms;
I drew them with human cords,
with bands of love;
I fostered them like one
who raises an infant to his cheeks;
Yet, though I stooped to feed my child,
they did not know that I was their healer.

My heart is overwhelmed,
my pity is stirred.
I will not give vent to my blazing anger,
I will not destroy Ephraim again;
For I am God and not a man,
the Holy One present among you;
I will not let the flames consume you.

The word of the Lord.

Readings from the New Testament

(Lectionary for Mass, nos. 996 and 998)

1 **161.** Romans 5:5-11

The love of God has been poured out into our hearts.

A reading from the Letter of Saint Paul to the Romans

Brothers and sisters:
Hope does not disappoint,
because the love of God has been poured out into our hearts
through the Holy Spirit who has been given to us.
For Christ, while we were still helpless,
died at the appointed time for the ungodly.
Indeed, only with difficulty does one die for a just person,
though perhaps for a good person
one might even find courage to die.
But God proves his love for us
in that while we were still sinners Christ died for us.
How much more then, since we are now justified by his Blood,
will we be saved through him from the wrath.
Indeed, if, while we were enemies,
we were reconciled to God through the death of his Son,
how much more, once reconciled,
will we be saved by his life.
Not only that,
but we also boast of God through our Lord Jesus Christ,
through whom we have now received reconciliation.

The word of the Lord.

2 162. Ephesians 1:3-10

In accord with the riches of his grace that he lavished upon us.

A reading from the Letter of Saint Paul to the Ephesians

Blessed be the God and Father of our Lord Jesus Christ,
who has blessed us in Christ
with every spiritual blessing in the heavens;
just as he has chosen us in him
before the foundation of the world
to be holy and blameless before him in love.
He destined us for adoption
to himself through Jesus Christ,
in accord with the good pleasure of his will,
to the praise of his glorious grace,
with which he favored us in the Beloved.

In him we have redemption through his blood,
the forgiveness of transgressions,
in accord with the riches of his grace
lavished on us in all wisdom and insight.
He has made known to us the mystery of his will
in accord with his good pleasure,
which he set forth in Christ as a plan,
a plan for the fullness of times,
to recapitulate all things in him,
things in heaven, and things on earth.

The word of the Lord.

3 163. Ephesians 3:8-12

To preach to the Gentiles the inscrutable riches of Christ.

A reading from the Letter of Saint Paul to the Ephesians

Brothers and sisters:
To me, the very least of all the holy ones, this grace was given,

to preach to the Gentiles the inscrutable riches of Christ,
and to bring to light for all what is the plan of the mystery
hidden from ages past in God who created all things,
so that the manifold wisdom of God
might now be made known through the Church
to the principalities and authorities in the heavens.
This was according to the eternal purpose
that he accomplished in Christ Jesus our Lord,
in whom we have boldness of speech
and confidence of access through faith in him.

The word of the Lord.

4 164. Ephesians 3:14-19

To know the love of Christ that surpasses all knowledge.

A reading from the Letter of Saint Paul to the Ephesians

Brothers and sisters:
I kneel before the Father,
from whom every family in heaven and on earth is named,
that he may grant you in accord with the riches of his glory
to be strengthened with power through his Spirit in the inner self,
and that Christ may dwell in your hearts through faith;
that you, rooted and grounded in love,
may have strength to comprehend with all the holy ones
what is the breadth and length and height and depth,
and to know the love of Christ that surpasses knowledge,
so that you may be filled with all the fullness of God.

The word of the Lord.

5 165. Philippians 1:8-11

With the affection of Christ Jesus.

A reading from the Letter of Saint Paul to the Philippians

Brothers and sisters:
God is my witness,
how I long for all of you with the affection of Christ Jesus.
And this is my prayer:
that your love may increase ever more and more
in knowledge and every kind of perception,
to discern what is of value,
so that you may be pure and blameless for the day of Christ,
filled with the fruit of righteousness
that comes through Jesus Christ
for the glory and praise of God.

The word of the Lord.

6 166. 1 John 4:7-16

Let us love one another.

A reading from the first Letter of Saint John

Beloved, let us love one another,
because love is of God;
everyone who loves is begotten by God and knows God.
Whoever is without love does not know God, for God is love.
In this way the love of God was revealed to us:
God sent his only-begotten Son into the world
so that we might have life through him.
In this is love:
not that we have loved God, but that he loved us
and sent his Son as expiation for our sins.

Beloved, if God so loved us,
we also must love one another.
No one has ever seen God.
Yet, if we love one another, God remains in us,
and his love is brought to perfection in us.

This is how we know that we remain in him and he in us,
that he has given us of his Spirit.
Moreover, we have seen and testify
that the Father sent his Son as savior of the world.
Whoever acknowledges that Jesus is the Son of God,
God remains in him and he in God.
We have come to know and to believe in the love God has for us.

God is love, and whoever remains in love
remains in God and God in him.

The word of the Lord.

7 167. Revelation 3:14b, 20-22

I will dine with him and he with me.

A reading from the Book of Revelation

"'The Amen, the faithful and true witness,
the source of God's creation, says this:

"'"Behold, I stand at the door and knock.
If anyone hears my voice and opens the door,
then I will enter his house and dine with him
and he with me.
I will give the victor the right to sit with me on my throne,
as I myself first won the victory
and sit with my Father on his throne.

"'"Whoever has ears ought to hear
what the Spirit says to the churches."'"

The word of the Lord.

8 168. Revelation 5:6-12

With your Blood you purchased us for God.

A reading from the Book of Revelation

I, John, saw standing in the midst of the throne
and the four living creatures and the elders
a Lamb that seemed to have been slain.
He had seven horns and seven eyes;
these are the seven spirits of God sent out into the whole world.
He came and received the scroll
from the right hand of the One who sat on the throne.
When he took it, the four living creatures and the twenty-four elders
fell down before the Lamb.
Each of the elders held a harp and gold bowls filled with incense,
which are the prayers of the holy ones.
They sang a new hymn:
"Worthy are you to receive the scroll
and to break open its seals,
for for you were slain
and with your Blood you have ransomed for God
those from every tongue and tribe,
and every people and nation:
and made them a kingdom and priests for our God,
and they shall reign on earth."
I looked again and heard the voices of many angels
who surrounded the throne
and the living creatures and the elders.
They were countless in number, and they cried out in a loud voice:
"Worthy is the Lamb that was slain
to receive power and riches and wisdom,
strength and honor, and glory and blessing."

The word of the Lord.

Responsorial Psalms

(*Lectionary for Mass*, no. 997)

1 169. Isaiah 12:2-3, 4bcd, 5-6

℟. (3) With joy will you draw water from the springs of salvation.

Behold, God is my salvation!
I will trust and will not be afraid,
for the Lord is my strength and my praise,
and he has been my salvation.
With joy will you draw water
from the springs of salvation.

℟. With joy will you draw water from the springs of salvation.

Give thanks to the Lord, invoke his name;
make known among the peoples his deeds;
proclaim that his name is exalted.

℟. With joy will you draw water from the springs of salvation.

Sing to the Lord for he has wrought wonders;
let this be known through all the earth.
Shout aloud and sing praise, you who dwell in Zion,
for great in your midst is the Holy One of Israel.

℟. With joy will you draw water from the springs of salvation.

2 170. Psalm 23 (22):1-3, 4, 5, 6

℟. (1) The Lord is my shepherd; there is nothing I shall want.

The Lord is my shepherd;
there is nothing I shall want.
Fresh and green are the pastures
where he gives me repose.

Near restful waters he leads me;
he revives my soul.
He guides me along the right path,
for the sake of his name.

℟. The Lord is my shepherd; there is nothing I shall want.

Though I should walk in the valley of the shadow of death,
no evil would I fear, for you are with me.
Your crook and your staff will give me comfort.

℟. The Lord is my shepherd; there is nothing I shall want.

You have prepared a table before me
in the sight of my foes.
My head you have anointed with oil;
my cup is overflowing.

℟. The Lord is my shepherd; there is nothing I shall want.

Surely goodness and mercy shall follow me
all the days of my life.
In the LORD's own house shall I dwell
for length of days unending.

℟. The Lord is my shepherd; there is nothing I shall want.

3 **171.** Psalm 25 (24):4-5ab, 6 and 7cd, 8-9, 10 and 14

℟. (6a) Remember your compassion, O Lord.

O LORD, make me know your ways.
Teach me your paths.
Guide me in your truth, and teach me;
for you are the God of my salvation.

℟. Remember your compassion, O Lord.

Remember your compassion, O Lord,
and your merciful love,
for they are from of old.
In your merciful love remember me,
because of your goodness, O Lord.

℟. Remember your compassion, O Lord.

Good and upright is the Lord;
therefore he shows the way to sinners.
He guides the humble in right judgment;
to the humble he teaches his way.

℟. Remember your compassion, O Lord.

All the Lord's paths are mercy and faithfulness,
for those who keep his covenant and commands.
The Lord's secret is for those who fear him;
to them he reveals his covenant.

℟. Remember your compassion, O Lord.

4 **172.** Psalm 33 (32):1-2, 4-5, 11-12, 18-19, 20-21

℟. (5b) The Lord's merciful love fills the earth.

Or:

℟. (Matthew 11:29b) Learn from me, for I am gentle and humble of heart.

Ring out your joy to the Lord, O you just;
for praise is fitting from the upright.
Give thanks to the Lord upon the harp;
with a ten-stringed lute sing him songs.

℟. The Lord's merciful love fills the earth.

Or:

℟. Learn from me, for I am gentle and humble of heart.

For the word of the Lord is upright,
and all his works to be trusted.
The Lord loves justice and right,
and his merciful love fills the earth.

℟. The Lord's merciful love fills the earth.

Or:

℟. Learn from me, for I am gentle and humble of heart.

The designs of the Lord stand forever,
the plans of his heart from age to age.
Blessed the nation whose God is the Lord,
the people he has chosen as his heritage.

℟. The Lord's merciful love fills the earth.

Or:

℟. Learn from me, for I am gentle and humble of heart.

Yes, the Lord's eyes are on those who fear him,
who hope in his merciful love,
to rescue their soul from death,
to keep them alive in famine.

℟. The Lord's merciful love fills the earth.

Or:

℟. Learn from me, for I am gentle and humble of heart.

Our soul is waiting for the Lord.
He is our help and our shield.
In him do our hearts find joy.
We trust in his holy name.

℟. The Lord's merciful love fills the earth.

Or:

℟. Learn from me, for I am gentle and humble of heart.

5 173. Psalm 34 (33):2-3, 4-5, 6-7, 8-9, 17-18, 19 and 23

℟. (9a) Taste and see that the Lord is good.

I will bless the Lord at all times,
praise of him is always in my mouth.
In the Lord my soul shall make its boast;
the humble shall hear and be glad.

℟. Taste and see that the Lord is good.

Glorify the Lord with me;
together let us praise his name.
I sought the Lord, and he answered me;
from all my terrors he set me free.

℟. Taste and see that the Lord is good.

Look toward him and be radiant;
let your faces not be abashed.
This lowly one called; the Lord heard,
and rescued him from all his distress.

℟. Taste and see that the Lord is good.

The angel of the Lord is encamped
around those who fear him, to rescue them.
Taste and see that the Lord is good.
Blessed the man who seeks refuge in him.

℟. Taste and see that the Lord is good.

The Lord turns his face against the wicked
to cut off their remembrance from the earth.
When the just one cries out, the Lord hears,
and rescues him in all his distress.

℟. Taste and see that the Lord is good.

The Lord is close to the brokenhearted;
those whose spirit is crushed he will save.
The Lord ransoms the souls of his servants.
All who trust in him shall not be condemned.

℟. Taste and see that the Lord is good.

6 **174.** Psalm 103 (102):1-2, 3-4, 6-7, 8 and 10

℟. (17) The mercy of the Lord is everlasting upon those who hold him in fear.

Bless the LORD, O my soul,
and all within me, his holy name.
Bless the LORD, O my soul,
and never forget all his benefits.

℟. The mercy of the Lord is everlasting upon those who hold him in fear.

It is the Lord who forgives all your sins,
who heals every one of your ills,
who redeems your life from the grave,
who crowns you with mercy and compassion.

℟. The mercy of the Lord is everlasting upon those who hold him in fear.

The LORD does deeds of justice,
gives full justice to all who are oppressed.
He made known his ways to Moses,
and his deeds to the children of Israel.

℟. The mercy of the Lord is everlasting upon those who hold him in fear.

The LORD is compassionate and gracious,
slow to anger and rich in mercy.
He does not treat us according to our sins,
nor repay us according to our faults.

℟. The mercy of the Lord is everlasting upon those who hold him in fear.

Alleluia Verses and Verses before the Gospel

(Lectionary for Mass, no. 999)

1 175. Cf. Matthew 11:25

**Blessed are you, Father, Lord of heaven and earth;
you have revealed to little ones the mysteries of the Kingdom.**

2 176. Matthew 11:28

**Come to me, all you who labor and are burdened,
and I will give you rest, says the Lord.**

3 177. Matthew 11:29ab

**Take my yoke upon you and learn from me,
for I am meek and humble of heart.**

4 178. John 10:14

**I am the good shepherd, says the Lord;
I know my sheep, and mine know me.**

5 179. John 15:9

**As the Father loves me, so I also love you.
Remain in my love.**

6 180. 1 John 4:10b

**God loved us and sent his Son
as expiation for our sins.**

Gospel Readings

(Lectionary for Mass, no. 1000)

1 181. Matthew 11:25-30

I am meek and humble of heart.

✠ **A reading from the holy Gospel according to Matthew**

At that time Jesus answered:
"I give praise to you, Father, Lord of heaven and earth,
for although you have hidden these things
from the wise and the learned
you have revealed them to the childlike.
Yes, Father, such has been your gracious will.
All things have been handed over to me by my Father.
No one knows the Son except the Father,
and no one knows the Father except the Son
and anyone to whom the Son wishes to reveal him."

"Come to me, all you who labor and are burdened,
and I will give you rest.
Take my yoke upon you and learn from me,
for I am meek and humble of heart;
and you will find rest for yourselves.
For my yoke is easy, and my burden light."

The Gospel of the Lord.

2 **182.** Luke 15:1-10

There will be joy in heaven over one sinner who repents.

✠ **A reading from the holy Gospel according to Luke**

Tax collectors and sinners were all drawing near to listen to Jesus,
but the Pharisees and scribes began to complain, saying,
"This man welcomes sinners and eats with them."
So to them Jesus addressed this parable.
"What man among you having a hundred sheep and losing one of them
would not leave the ninety-nine in the desert
and go after the lost one until he finds it?
And when he does find it,
he sets it on his shoulders with great joy
and, upon his arrival home,
he calls together his friends and neighbors and says to them,
'Rejoice with me because I have found my lost sheep.'
I tell you, in just the same way
there will be more joy in heaven over one sinner who repents
than over ninety-nine righteous people
who have no need of repentance.

"Or what woman having ten coins and losing one
would not light a lamp and sweep the house,
searching carefully until she finds it?
And when she does find it,
she calls together her friends and neighbors
and says to them,
'Rejoice with me because I have found the coin that I lost.'
In just the same way, I tell you,
there will be rejoicing among the angels of God
over one sinner who repents."

The Gospel of the Lord.

3 **183.** Luke 15:1-3, 11-32

Now we must celebrate and rejoice because your brother was dead and has come back to life.

✠ **A reading from the holy Gospel according to Luke**

Tax collectors and sinners were all drawing near to listen to Jesus,
but the Pharisees and scribes began to complain, saying,
"This man welcomes sinners and eats with them."
So to them Jesus addressed this parable.
"A man had two sons, and the younger son said to his father,
'Father give me the share of your estate that should come to me.'
So the father divided the property between them.
After a few days, the younger son collected all his belongings
and set off to a distant country
where he squandered his inheritance on a life of dissipation.
When he had freely spent everything,
a severe famine struck that country,
and he found himself in dire need.
So he hired himself out to one of the local citizens
who sent him to his farm to tend the swine.
And he longed to eat his fill of the pods on which the swine fed,
but nobody gave him any.
Coming to his senses he thought,
'How many of my father's hired workers
have more than enough food to eat,
but here am I, dying from hunger.
I shall get up and go to my father and I shall say to him,
"Father, I have sinned against heaven and against you.

I no longer deserve to be called your son;
treat me as you would treat one of your hired workers."'
So he got up and went back to his father.
While he was still a long way off,
his father caught sight of him, and was filled with compassion.
He ran to his son, embraced him and kissed him.
His son said to him,
'Father, I have sinned against heaven and against you;
I no longer deserve to be called your son.'
But his father ordered his servants,
'Quickly bring the finest robe and put it on him;
put a ring on his finger and sandals on his feet.
Take the fattened calf and slaughter it.
Then let us celebrate with a feast,
because this son of mine was dead, and has come to life again;
he was lost, and has been found.'
Then the celebration began.
Now the older son had been out in the field
and, on his way back, as he neared the house,
he heard the sound of music and dancing.
He called one of the servants and asked what this might mean.
The servant said to him,
'Your brother has returned
and your father has slaughtered the fattened calf
because he has him back safe and sound.'
He became angry,
and when he refused to enter the house,
his father came out and pleaded with him.
He said to his father in reply,
'Look, all these years I served you
and not once did I disobey your orders;

yet you never gave me even a young goat to feast on with my friends.
But when your son returns
who swallowed up your property with prostitutes,
for him you slaughter the fattened calf.'
He said to him,
'My son, you are here with me always;
everything I have is yours.
But now we must celebrate and rejoice,
because your brother was dead and has come to life again;
he was lost and has been found.'"

The Gospel of the Lord.

4 184. John 10:11-18

A good shepherd lays down his life for the sheep.

✠ A reading from the holy Gospel according to John

Jesus said:
"I am the good shepherd.
A good shepherd lays down his life for the sheep.
A hired man, who is not a shepherd
and whose sheep are not his own,
sees a wolf coming and leaves the sheep and runs away,
and the wolf catches and scatters them.
This is because he works for pay and has no concern for the sheep.
I am the good shepherd,
and I know mine and mine know me,
just as the Father knows me and I know the Father;
and I will lay down my life for the sheep.
I have other sheep that do not belong to this fold.
These also I must lead, and they will hear my voice,
and there will be one flock, one shepherd.

This is why the Father loves me,
because I lay down my life in order to take it up again.
No one takes it from me, but I lay it down on my own.
I have power to lay it down, and power to take it up again.
This command I have received from my Father."

The Gospel of the Lord.

5 185. John 15:1-8

Remain in me as I remain in you.

✠ A reading from the holy Gospel according to John

Jesus said to his disciples:
"I am the true vine, and my Father is the vine grower.
He takes away every branch in me that does not bear fruit,
and every one that does he prunes so that it bears more fruit.
You are already pruned because of the word that I spoke to you.
Remain in me, as I remain in you.
Just as a branch cannot bear fruit on its own
unless it remains on the vine,
so neither can you unless you remain in me.
I am the vine, you are the branches.
Whoever remains in me and I in him will bear much fruit,
because without me you can do nothing.
Anyone who does not remain in me
will be thrown out like a branch and wither;
people will gather them and throw them into a fire
and they will be burned.
If you remain in me and my words remain in you,
ask for whatever you want and it will be done for you.
By this is my Father glorified,
that you bear much fruit and become my disciples."

The Gospel of the Lord.

6 **186.** John 15:9-17

Love one another as I love you.

✠ **A reading from the holy Gospel according to John**

Jesus said to his disciples:
"As the Father loves me, so I also love you.
Remain in my love.
If you keep my commandments, you will remain in my love,
just as I have kept my Father's commandments
and remain in his love.

"I have told you this so that my joy may be in you
and your joy may be complete.
This is my commandment: love one another as I love you.
No one has greater love than this,
to lay down one's life for one's friends.
You are my friends if you do what I command you.
I no longer call you slaves,
because a slave does not know what his master is doing.
I have called you friends,
because I have told you everything I have heard from my Father.
It was not you who chose me, but I who chose you
and appointed you to go and bear fruit that will remain,
so that whatever you ask the Father in my name he may give you.
This I command you: love one another."

The Gospel of the Lord.

7 **187.** John 17:20-26

You loved them as you loved me.

✠ **A reading from the holy Gospel according to John**

Jesus raised his eyes to heaven and said:
"Holy Father, I pray not only for these,
but also for those who will believe in me through their word,
so that they may all be one,
as you, Father, are in me and I in you,
that they also may be in us,
that the world may believe that you sent me.
And I have given them the glory you gave me,
so that they may be one, as we are one,
I in them and you in me,
that they may be brought to perfection as one,
that the world may know that you sent me,
and that you loved them even as you loved me.
Father, they are your gift to me.
I wish that where I am they also may be with me,
that they may see my glory that you gave me,
because you loved me before the foundation of the world.
Righteous Father, the world also does not know you,
but I know you, and they know that you sent me.
I made known to them your name and I will make it known,
that the love with which you loved me
may be in them and I in them."

The Gospel of the Lord.

8 **188.** John 19:31-37

One of the soldiers thrust his lance into his side
and immediately Blood and water flowed out.

✠ **A reading from the holy Gospel according to John**

Since it was preparation day,
in order that the bodies might not remain on the cross
on the sabbath,
for the sabbath day of that week was a solemn one,
the Jews asked Pilate that their legs be broken
and they be taken down.
So the soldiers came and broke the legs of the first
and then of the other one who was crucified with Jesus.
But when they came to Jesus and saw that he was
already dead,
they did not break his legs,
but one soldier thrust his lance into his side,
and immediately Blood and water flowed out.
An eyewitness has testified, and his testimony is true;
he knows that he is speaking the truth,
so that you also may come to believe.
For this happened so that the Scripture passage might
be fulfilled:
Not a bone of it will be broken.
And again another passage says:
They will look upon him whom they have pierced.

The Gospel of the Lord.

II. Another Form of Greeting

189.

**Grace to you and peace from God our Father
and the Lord Jesus Christ.**

All reply:

Blessed be the God and Father of our Lord Jesus Christ.

Or:

And with your spirit.

III. Other Forms of the Penitential Act

190. The minister invites the faithful to repentance:

Brethren (Brothers and sisters), let us acknowledge our sins, and so prepare ourselves to participate in this sacred celebration.

A brief pause for silence follows. Then the minister says:

Have mercy on us, O Lord.

All reply:

For we have sinned against you.

Minister:

Show us, O Lord, your mercy.

All reply:

And grant us your salvation.

The minister concludes:

**May almighty God have mercy on us,
forgive us our sins,
and bring us to everlasting life.**

All reply:

Amen.

191. The minister invites the faithful to repentance:

Brethren (Brothers and sisters), let us acknowledge our sins, and so prepare ourselves to participate in this sacred celebration.

And a brief pause for silence follows. The minister, or one of those present, then says the following or other invocations with Kyrie, eleison (Lord, have mercy):

You gained salvation for us by your Paschal Mystery:

Lord, have mercy. Or: **Kyrie, eleison.**

All:

Lord, have mercy. Or: Kyrie, eleison.

Minister:

You never cease to renew among us the wonders of your Passion:

Christ, have mercy. Or: **Christe, eleison.**

All:

Christ, have mercy. Or: Christe, eleison.

Minister:

You make us sharers in your Paschal Sacrifice
through the reception of your Body:

Lord, have mercy. Or: **Kyrie, eleison.**

All:

Lord, have mercy. Or: Kyrie, eleison.

The minister concludes:

May almighty God have mercy on us,
forgive us our sins,
and bring us to everlasting life.

All reply:

Amen.

IV. Hymns

192. Pange, lingua (Sing, My Tongue, the Hidden Mystery)

At the blessing that concludes adoration, especially when this occurs in a shorter form, singing may be confined to the last part of the hymn **Pange, lingua** (**Sing, my tongue, the hidden mystery**), beginning with the words **Tantum ergo** (**Let us, therefore, bow and worship**).

1. Sing, my tongue, the_ hid - den mys - t'ry of_ Christ's Bod - y
2. Born for us and giv - en to_ us Son of Mar - y,
3. On the night of_ that Last Sup - per feast - ing with his
4. Word made flesh, true bread from heav - en, by_ a word, made
* 5. Let us, there - fore, bow and wor - ship such a won - drous
6. To the Fa - ther, un - be - got - ten, and the Sole - be -

1. glo - ri - fied,_ and his Pre - cious Blood most ho - ly,
2. Vir - gin pure,_ in the world he lived a - mong us,
3. cho - sen friends, he o - beyed the law com - plete - ly
4. bread his Flesh, pur - est wine Christ's Blood be - com - ing,
5. Sac - ra - ment; let the an - cient law and cus - tom
6. got - ten Son,_ be sal - va - tion, bless - ing, hon - or,

1. shed in ran - som for the world, of - fered by the
2. sowed as seeds the word of truth; then the sea - son
3. in the food and drink pre - scribed; then he gave his
4. though our sense can - not per - ceive; faith a - lone brings
5. to a new - er rite now yield; let our faith sup -
6. ju - bi - la - tion, pow'r, and praise; to the One from

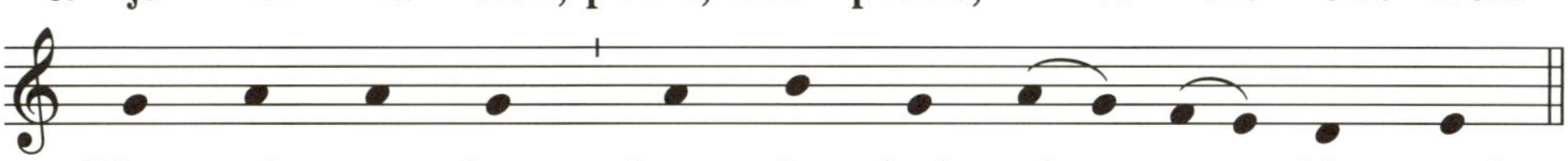

1. King of na - tions, born the fruit of___ no - ble womb.
2. of his so - journ with a won - drous rite_ he closed.
3. twelve A - pos - tles with his hands him - self_ as food.
4. full as - sur - ance to the pure and_ faith - ful heart.
5. ply con - vic - tion where the sens - es___ tire_ and fail.
6. both pro - ceed - ing e - qual glo - ry___ and_ re - nown.

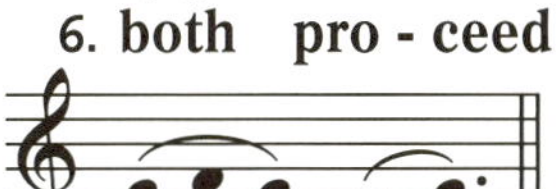

6. A - men.

193. Sacris sollemniis (Let Our Joys Magnify Sacred Solemnities)

1. Let_ our joys mag - ni - fy sa - cred so - lem - ni - ties,
2. Christ on that bless - ed_ night, at his last Pas - chal Meal,
3. Then for the_ frail_ and_ weak he gave his Flesh as food,
4. Christ in - sti - tut - ed_ thus this ver - y sac - ri - fice,
5. Bread of the_ an - gel_ hosts now is made bread for us,
6. O___ God - head, Three in__ One, hear us, we beg of you:

1. prais - es re - ech - o - ing_ from the heart's hid - den depth;
2. gave his dis - ci - ples there, as__ we re - call_ in faith,
3. and for the_ sor - row - ful_ he_ gave his Blood as drink,
4. grant-ing to___ priests a - lone pow - er to of - fer it,
5. heav - en - ly___ bread from God, truth of all proph - e - cies,
6. as we a - dore you, Lord, so__ come and vis - it us,

1. let the old_ pass a - way, all__ things be__ new a - gain,
2. lamb and un - leav - ened bread, food by the_ Law be - stowed
3. say - ing: Re - ceive this cup, which I hand on to_ you;
4. by his will_ and his charge mak - ing them fit to_ act,
5. O mar - vel,_ won - drous gift! Who may con - sume the_ Lord?
6. lead us a - long your paths, where our hearts long to_ go,

1. hearts and voic - es__ and ev - 'ry work.
2. on___ our fa - thers of an - cient days.
3. take_ this, all___ of__ you, drink from it.__
4. to___ re - ceive,_ and_ to oth - ers give.
5. Low - ly ser - vants and poor of heart.
6. to___ that light_ where you live_ and reign. A - men.

194. Verbum supernum (The Word Proceeding from on High)

1. The Word___ pro - ceed - ing__ from on high, though leav - ing
2. Though one____ dis - ci - ple__would, for death, be - tray him
3. Be - neath___ a__ dou - ble__ form he gave to them his
4. He gave___ him - self_ in___ birth as friend, in feast - ing
*5. O Vic - tim bring - ing__ sav - ing grace, who o - pen
6. To you____ be_ ev - er - last - ing praise and glo - ry,

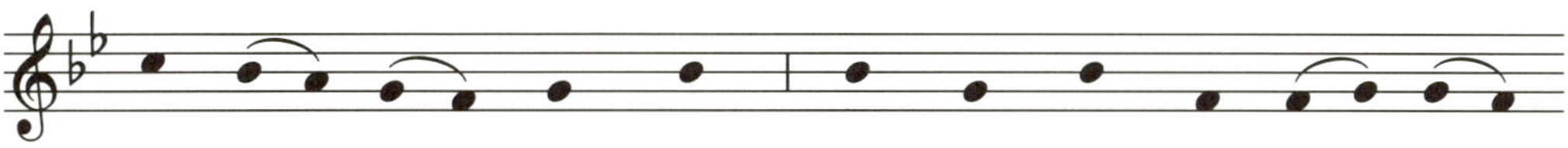

1. not the_ Fa - ther's right, went forth to do his_ work
2. to his_ en - vious foes, to his dis - ci - ples_ first_
3. ho - ly__ flesh and blood to be the per - fect_ food
4. as our_ liv - ing food, in dy - ing as our_ ran -
5. wide the_ gate_ of heav'n: our foes as - sail and_ press
6. One and_ Tri - une Lord, who grant us life that_ knows

1. on earth and reached the_ eve - ning_ of his life.
2. he chose to give_ him - self_ as__ food of life.
3. that feeds the two - fold_ sub - stance of our frame.
4. som paid, in reign - ing_ as___ our_ great re - ward.
5. us hard; give us___ your strength, bring us your aid.
6. no end, for ev - er__ in___ our_ heav'n - ly home.

6. A - men.

195. Iesu, nostra redemptio (O Jesus, Our Redeeming Lord)

1. O Je - sus, our__ re - deem-ing_ Lord, our great-est
2. What lov - ing mer - cy mas - tered you, that you_ should
3. For us____ you breached the walls of__ hell and ran - somed
4. May this___ same love_ com - pel_ you_ still to o - ver -
5. Lord Je - sus, be___ all joy_ for_ us, for you_ shall

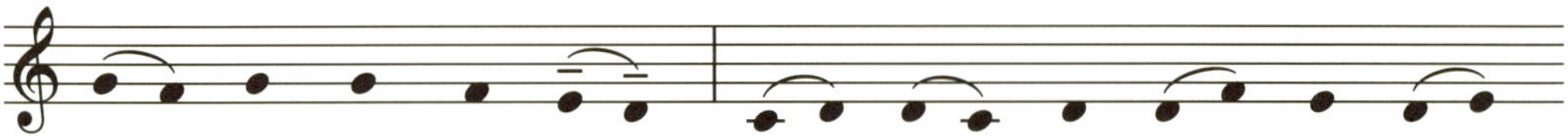

1. love_ and all de - sire,_ true_ God, Cre - a - tor of__
2. bear our griev-ous sins_ and_ suf - fer cruel and bit -
3. all__ your cap - tives there; as__ vic - tor at__ the Fa -
4. come our e - vil deeds, to__ par - don us__ and grant
5. be__ our great re - ward; may all__ our glo - ry be__

1. all things, true Man_ be - yond the end_ of___ time,
2. ter death to res - cue us__ from death's do - main?
3. ther's right, in no - ble tri - umph you_ pre - side.
4. that we may gaze_ in won - der at__ your_ face.
5. in you through end - less ag - es ev - er - more.

5. A - men.

196. Æterne rex altissime (Eternal King and God Most High)

1. E - ter - nal_ King and_ God most high, Re-deem-er
2. You mount__ the_ ho - ly__ judg-ment seat, es - tab-lished
3. That all______ in__ heav-en__ and on earth and in the
4. The an - gels_ trem-ble__ as they watch the mor-tal
5. O Christ,__ you_ are_ our_ last-ing joy, our sure, a -
6. And so______ with hum-ble_prayer we ask that you for -
7. That when___ the_ clouds grow red with dawn and you, the
8. To you,____ Lord Je - sus,_ glo - ry be, who now as -

1. of all__ faith-ful souls, in you the pow'r of__ death
2. at the_ Fa - ther's right, re - ceiv-ing pow'r to__ rule_
3. neth-er - world be - low, the three-fold u - ni - verse
4. or - der_ o - ver-turned: in flesh the sin, in__ flesh
5. bid-ing_ rec - om-pense, who rule the fab - ric_ of__
6. give us__ all__ our faults, and by your heav'n-ly__ gift
7. Judge, ap - pear_ in light, you may re - mit the_ debt
8. cend to__ heav-en's height, with God the Fa - ther, ev -

1. is crushed, and tri - umph shown in__ gifts of grace.
2. all things, di - vine,_ not_ hu - man, sov-'reign - ty,
3. you made, should bend the_ knee in__ trib - ute now.
4. the cure, in flesh_ the_ reign of__ God the Word.
5. this world, yet far__ sur - pass_ all__ earth-ly joys.
6. of grace lift up__ our_ hearts to__ you on high,
7. we owe and so__ re - store the_ crown we lost.
8. er blest, and lov - ing_ Spir - it,__ ev - er one.

8. A - men.

197. Lauda, Sion

This Sequence is sung either in its entirety or in a shorter form, beginning at the words Ecce panis (Lo! the angel's food is given).

Laud, O Zion, your salvation,
Laud with hymns of exultation,
Christ, your king and shepherd true:

Bring him all the praise you know,
He is more than you bestow.
Never can you reach his due.

Special theme for glad thanksgiving
Is the quick'ning and the living
Bread today before you set:

From his hands of old partaken,
As we know, by faith unshaken,
Where the Twelve at supper met.

Full and clear ring out your chanting,
Joy nor sweetest grace be wanting,
From your heart let praises burst:

For today the feast is holden,
When the institution olden
Of that supper was rehearsed.

Here the new law's new oblation,
By the new king's revelation,
Ends the form of ancient rite:

Now the new the old effaces,
Truth away the shadow chases,
Light dispels the gloom of night.

What he did at supper seated,
Christ ordained to be repeated,
His memorial ne'er to cease:

And his rule for guidance taking,
Bread and wine we hallow, making
Thus our sacrifice of peace.

This the truth each Christian learns,
Bread into his flesh he turns,
To his precious blood the wine:

Sight has fail'd, nor thought conceives,
But a dauntless faith believes,
Resting on a pow'r divine.

Here beneath these signs are hidden
Priceless things to sense forbidden;
Signs, not things are all we see:

Blood is poured and flesh is broken,
Yet in either wondrous token
Christ entire we know to be.

Whoso of this food partakes,
Does not rend the Lord nor breaks;
Christ is whole to all that taste:

Thousands are, as one, receivers,
One, as thousands of believers,
Eats of him who cannot waste.

Bad and good the feast are sharing,
Of what divers dooms preparing,
Endless death, or endless life.

Life to these, to those damnation,
See how like participation
Is with unlike issues rife.

When the sacrament is broken,
Doubt not, but believe 'tis spoken,
That each sever'd outward token
doth the very whole contain.

Nought the precious gift divides,
Breaking but the sign betides
Jesus still the same abides,
still unbroken does remain.

*Lo! the angel's food is given
To the pilgrim who has striven;
See the children's bread from heaven,
which on dogs may not be spent.

Truth the ancient types fulfilling,
Isaac bound, a victim willing,
Paschal lamb, its lifeblood spilling,
manna to the fathers sent.

Very bread, good shepherd, tend us,
Jesu, of your love befriend us,
You refresh us, you defend us,
Your eternal goodness send us
In the land of life to see.

You who all things can and know,
Who on earth such food bestow,
Grant us with your saints, though lowest,
Where the heav'nly feast you show,
Fellow heirs and guests to be.
Amen. Alleluia.

198. Adoro devote

Hidden here before me, Lord, I worship you,
hidden in these symbols, yet completely true.
Lord, my soul surrenders, longing to obey,
and in contemplation wholly faints away.

Seeing, touching, tasting: these are all deceived;
only through the hearing can it be believed.
Nothing is more certain: Christ has told me so;
what the Truth has uttered, I believe and know.

Only God was hidden when you came to die;
human nature also here escapes the eye.
Both are my profession, both are my belief;
bring me to your Kingdom, like the dying thief.

I am not like Thomas, who could see and touch;
though your wounds are hidden, I believe as much.

Let me say so boldly, meaning what I say,
loving you and trusting, now and every day.

Record of the Passion when the Lamb was slain,
living bread that brings us back to life again,
feed me with your presence, make me live on you;
let that lovely fragrance fill me through and through.

Once a nesting pelican gashed herself to blood
for the preservation of her starving brood;
now heal me with your blood, take away my guilt;
all the world is ransomed if one drop is spilt.

Jesus, for the present seen as through a mask,
give me what I thirst for, give me what I ask:
let me see your glory in a blaze of light,
and instead of blindness give me, Lord, my sight. Amen.

199. Ubi caritas

Ant. Where true charity is dwelling, God is present there.
℣. By the love of Christ we have been brought together:
℣. let us find in him our gladness and our pleasure;
℣. may we love him and revere him, God the living,
℣. and in love respect each other with sincere hearts.

Ant. Where true charity is dwelling, God is present there.
℣. So when we as one are gathered all together,
℣. let us strive to keep our minds free of division;
℣. may there be an end to malice, strife and quarrels,
℣. and let Christ our God be dwelling here among us.

Ant. Where true charity is dwelling, God is present there.
℣. May your face thus be our vision, bright in glory,
℣. Christ our God, with all the blessed Saints in heaven:
℣. such delight is pure and faultless, joy unbounded,
℣. which endures through countless ages world without end. Amen.

Other liturgical songs found in the Liturgy of the Hours that celebrate the Paschal Mystery of Christ may be used if appropriate.

V. Antiphons

200. O sacred banquet, in which Christ is received:
the memory of his Passion is renewed,
the mind is filled with grace,
and a pledge of future glory is given to us.

201. How delightful your spirit, O Lord!
To show your sweetness to your children,
you fill the hungry with good things,
offering them the sweetest bread from heaven,
and sending the rich and haughty away empty.

202. Hail, true Body, born of the Virgin Mary,
who truly suffered, was sacrificed on the Cross for us,
from whose pierced side flowed water and blood.
Be for us a foretaste of heaven in the final trial of death,
O sweet Jesus, O loving Jesus, O Jesus Son of Mary.

203. I am the living bread that came down from heaven;
whoever eats of this bread will live for ever;
and the bread that I will give
is my flesh for the life of the world.

VI. Responsories

204. While they were at supper,
Jesus took bread, blessed and broke it,
and gave it to his disciples, saying:
* Take and eat: this is my Body.

℣. The men of my dwelling place have said:
Who will give us his flesh,
that we may be satisfied?
* Take and eat: this is my Body.

205. I am the bread of life:
your ancestors ate manna in the wilderness and are dead;
* This is the bread that comes down from heaven,
so that whoever eats of it may not die.

℣. I am the living bread that came down from heaven:
whoever eats of this bread will live for ever.
* This is the bread that comes down from heaven,
so that whoever eats of it may not die.

206. Recognize in the bread that which hung on the Cross;
in the chalice that which flowed from his side.
Take, therefore, and eat the Body of Christ;
take and drink the Blood of Christ.
* Now, therefore, you are the members of Christ.

℣. Lest you be scattered, eat what binds you together;
lest you feel yourselves to be worthless,
drink the price of your salvation.
* Now, therefore, you are the members of Christ.

207. Though many, we are one bread, one body,
* for we all partake of the one Bread and one Chalice.

℣. In your goodness, O God, you provided for the poor,
you give the desolate a home to dwell in.
* for we all partake in the one Bread and one Chalice.

208. A certain man held a great feast,
and sent his servant at the time of the feast to tell those invited to come,
* for everything is prepared.

℣. Come, eat my food and drink the wine which I have mixed for you,
* for everything is prepared.

209. The living Father sent me, and I live because of the Father:
*** and whoever feeds on me shall have life because of me.**

℣. The Lord fed him with the bread of life and understanding:
*** and whoever feeds on me shall have life because of me.**

VII. Prayers after Communion

210. O God, who have accomplished the work of human redemption
through the Paschal Mystery of your Only Begotten Son,
graciously grant that we, who confidently proclaim,
under sacramental signs, the Death and Resurrection of Christ,
may experience continued increase of your saving grace.
Through Christ our Lord.

211. Pour on us, O Lord, the Spirit of your love,
and in your kindness
make those you have nourished
by this one heavenly Bread
one in mind and heart.
Through Christ our Lord.

212. May sharing at the heavenly table
sanctify us, Lord, we pray,
so that through the Body and Blood of Christ
the whole family of believers may be bound together.
Through Christ our Lord.

213. **Replenished by the food of spiritual nourishment,**
we humbly beseech you, O Lord,
that, through our partaking in this mystery,
you may teach us to judge wisely the things of earth
and hold firm to the things of heaven.
Through Christ our Lord.

214. **As we receive these glorious mysteries,**
we make thanksgiving to you, O Lord,
for allowing us while still on earth
to be partakers even now of the things of heaven.
Through Christ our Lord.

215. **Humbly we ask you, almighty God,**
be graciously pleased to grant
that those you renew with your Sacraments
may also serve with lives pleasing to you.
Through Christ our Lord.

216. **O God, who have willed that we be partakers**
in the one Bread and the one Chalice,
grant us, we pray, so to live
that, made one in Christ,
we may joyfully bear fruit
for the salvation of the world.
Through Christ our Lord.

217. **Renewed by this bread from the heavenly table,**
we beseech you, Lord,
that, being the food of charity,
it may confirm our hearts
and stir us to serve you in our neighbor.
Through Christ our Lord.

218. Nourished by this sacred gift, O Lord,
we give you thanks and beseech your mercy,
that, by the pouring forth of your Spirit,
the grace of integrity may endure
in those your heavenly power has entered.
Through Christ our Lord.

219. Renewed by the one Bread
we humbly beseech you, O Lord,
that, confirmed in your love,
we may walk in newness of life.
Through Christ our Lord.

Easter Time:

220. Pour out on us, O Lord, the Spirit of your love,
and in your kindness
make those you have nourished
by this paschal Sacrament
one in mind and heart.
Through Christ our Lord.

221. We pray, O Lord,
that the reverent reception of the Sacrament of your Son
may cleanse us from our old ways
and transform us into a new creation.
Through Christ our Lord.

222. Almighty ever-living God,
who restore us to eternal life
in the Resurrection of Christ,
increase in us, we pray, the fruits of this paschal Sacrament
and pour into our hearts the strength of this saving food.
Through Christ our Lord.

223. Another prayer after Viaticum:

O Lord, eternal health and salvation
of those who believe in you,
grant, we pray, that your servant N.,
renewed by heavenly food and drink,
may safely reach your Kingdom of light and life.
Through Christ our Lord.

VIII. Prayers at Benediction of the Most Blessed Sacrament

224. **Lord God, we believe and confess**
that Jesus Christ, who was born for us of the Virgin Mary
and suffered on the Cross,
is present in the Sacrament;
grant that we may draw from this divine wellspring
the gift of eternal salvation.
Through Christ our Lord.

225. **Grant us, we pray, Lord God,**
to celebrate with worthy praises
the Lamb who was slain for us
and is hidden in this Sacrament,
so that we may be worthy to contemplate him
when he is revealed in glory.
Who lives and reigns for ever and ever.

226. **O God,**
who have given us the true Bread from heaven,
grant, we pray,
that by the power of this spiritual food,
we may always live in you
and rise in glory on the Last Day.
Through Christ our Lord.

227. **Enlighten our hearts, O Lord,**
with the light of faith
and kindle in them the fire of love,
that we may confidently adore in spirit and in truth
him whom we acknowledge in this Sacrament
to be our Lord and God.
Who lives and reigns for ever and ever.

228. **May the Sacraments**
by which you have been pleased to restore us, Lord,
fill our hearts with the sweetness of your love
and make us long for the unfathomable riches of your Kingdom.
Through Christ our Lord.

229. **O God, who by the Paschal Mystery of Christ**
have redeemed the whole world,
preserve in us the work of your mercy,
so that, ever honoring the mystery of our salvation,
we may merit to obtain its fruits.
Through Christ our Lord.